ESSENTIAL SH!T
GW00359546
STUFF YOU SHOULD KNOW HOW TO DO BUT PROBABLY DON'T
The manual no REAL MAN should be without
D&C
David and Charles

A DAVID & CHARLES BOOK

David & Charles is an imprint of F&W Media International, LTD
Brunel House, Forde Close, Newton Abbot, TQ12 4PU, UK

F&W Media International, LTD is a subsidiary of F+W Media, Inc.
4700 East Galbraith Road, Cincinnati, OH 45236

First published in the UK in 2011

The material in this book has been previously published in *How to Back Up a Trailer*, published by Adams Media, 2008.

A catalogue record for this book is available from the British Library.

ISBN-13: 978-1-4463-0042-8 paperback
ISBN-10: 1-4463-0042-0 paperback

Printed in China by RR Donnelley
for F&W Media International LTD,
Brunel House, Forde Close, Newton Abbot, TQ12 4PU, UK

10 9 8 7 6 5 4 3 2 1

Senior Acquisitions Editor: Freya Dangerfield
Assistant Editor: Felicity Barr
Project Editor: Stuart Robertson
Proofreader: Freya Dangerfield
Senior Designer: Jodie Lystor
Senior Production Controller: Kelly Smith

Contents

Acknowledgements

I'd like to thank the following people for their help with this book:

To Justin Neudahl, longtime supporter, an invaluable first reader, and duck-blind buddy, I owe many thanks, most of all for being a friend. The other guys and gals from whom I've learned "real-guy" stuff could fill up pages, but I'd especially like to thank Adam Janke, Willy Janke, the Ehnes clan, Robert "Button Buck" Anderson, Wayno Langley, Don "Corky" Hemsworth, Kurt Johnson, Todd Blom, Rick McRae, and Al Price. To my sisters, Suzie Janke and Becca Karppinen, and my mother, Nita Anderson, thanks for everything, and especially for putting up with "Cliff." You know what I mean.

Sometimes the simplest things take on a new wonder when you show them to, or experience them with, fresh eyes: Kolten, Kourtney, Kody, Krystal, Drew, Lindsey, and Joey, you guys (and girls) rock. I'd also like to thank Duane Johnson and Gary Wentz at *The Family Handyman* magazine, two of the nicest guys out there. Their guidance in how-to writing was indispensable. Thanks many times over to Jill Alexander and Katrina Schroeder for their enthusiasm and help in shaping an idea into a book.

This book would not have happened without Jim Donovan, one hell of a fine literary agent and person. Many thanks, chief.

And most importantly, I'd like to express my gratitude to my wife, Tina Lee, for keeping an eye on our wonderful sons, Tyler and Carter, while I was writing, for always encouraging me, and for being the best wife a guy could ask for. Love ya, hon.

This book is dedicated in loving memory of my father, Bill Anderson, who left this world a few years back. He is still with me, though . . . and no doubt laughing, in his good way, when I'm being a knucklehead about one thing or another.

Miss you, Dad.

William "Bill" Anderson. 1941–2004

Introduction

Here's a shocker: blokes don't know everything. In fact, when it comes to supposedly 'innate' bloke knowledge, a lot of us feel like we're holding a weak torch in a big, dark garage, just trying to work out how to open up the bloody overhead door.

We stand, as the saying goes, on the shoulders of giants. Our mechanically-adept forefathers left a world of complicated machinery in their wake, willing us an incredible amount of 'should-know' technical detail, on everything from electrical circuitry to ballistics to mechanical engineering. Along with the practical stuff, we also inherited arcane yet still-powerful rules of sportsmanship and hard-nosed etiquette, with nuances and intricacies as unfathomable as three-fork dinner settings.

But those geniuses didn't leave us a guidebook – or even an instruction manual. No wonder we feel lost from time to time. It's hard to admit this, especially if you're a bloke. We like and admire those handy types who can fix a leaking sump or rewire a faulty light switch, those practical men who know how to clean a fish and make a smokeless fire to cook it over. We want to be like them, to have that natural confidence that shows through so clearly, even when – perhaps especially when – things start going to pot.

Well, learning things the hard way can be both entertaining and memorable. Yet I've suffered enough broken bones and bruises to my ego to realize that sometimes the hard way is, well, just hard, with no redeeming value. It doesn't hurt to take a little advice now and then, because this isn't stuff we're born with. But it is stuff you really should know.

The trouble is, there are many specialists in today's world but few general handymen. And while nobody will fault you for not knowing how to power down a nuclear reactor or completely re-programme your knackered PC, you'll be judged by a different standard when the car stalls, the house goes dark, or – God forbid – the beer fridge quits working. It is here, on the verges of dark roads and the cellars of old houses, that the tips in this book will become invaluable.

So sit back, crack open a cold one, and we'll... what's that? No bottle opener? Christ no, don't put it back. We'll get her open for you.

ON THE ROAD

Push start a car

A stalled manual gearbox car with starting problems doesn't necessarily have to be jump-started or fixed on the spot. All you need is a little bit of juice in the battery, a clear stretch of road, and a little help.

Hook your car up to another car with a tow strap or get some burly passers-by to put their backs into it (ask the ladies to remove their heels first), turn on the key, and put the car into second gear. Leave the clutch in, and have the towing car or hired muscle pull or push you until you reach a speed that would normally be a bit too high for second gear, then 'pop the clutch' – that is, let out the clutch in one go. The car will jerk as the transmission is engaged, which should cause your engine to turn over and start. Make sure you push the clutch back in right away and apply the accelerator. This is best done downhill and away from oncoming traffic, for obvious reasons.

The target speed depends on the specific engine size and gear ratio of the stalled vehicle, but a general rule of thumb is a target speed of ten to twelve times the gear you're in. If you're going a lot faster than you normally would for the gear you're in (e.g. 40 miles an hour and you pop the clutch in second gear) you're going to get one hell of a jolt, and it might even ruin the gearbox. It's always best to err on the low side.

If you had a dead battery, be sure to keep the car running for at least ten minutes so the alternator can recharge the battery. If it wouldn't start because of a mechanical or electrical problem you'll need to get it fixed right away – or spend the rest of your life parking on hilltops.

Change a spare tyre

Personally I like my spare tyre. It's had a lot of time and effort invested in it which it would be a shame to write off at the gym. But let's ignore that for now and instead locate each component of your tyre-changing system. Every car should have a jack, tyre ratchet or iron, and a fully inflated spare tyre. If the spare tyre isn't somewhere obvious, such as under the carpet in the boot, it's probably held in place underneath the car by a cable. Obviously a dark hard shoulder somewhere isn't the most sensible place to track down these things; your driveway on a Sunday afternoon will be easier.

Experiment with the ratchet and jack until you can tighten/loosen or lower/raise each one respectively. Often the ratchet also operates the jack – there's usually an instruction manual in the spare-tyre or jack holder. The ratchet may come in two pieces, with a long 'socket bar' that slides through the ratchet.

Mechanics often over-tighten lug nuts to prevent liability issues, sometimes far past required levels. Since you've got everything out, pop off the hubcap and try to loosen one of the lug nuts. If it won't turn, try sliding a section of metal pipe over the end of the ratchet handle. This is called a cheater pipe, and the technique can be used on any wrench or ratchet to increase leverage. If the lug nut turns with the cheater pipe, be sure to stash the pipe somewhere in the car, preferably next to the jack.

If the lug nuts still won't turn, bring your car into the dealer or a mechanic and ask them to loosen the lug nuts to an acceptable pressure, somewhere around 150 foot-pounds of torque. The exact number should be in your owner's manual. Of course, you're better off too tight than too loose, but it's no good being stuck somewhere with a flat tyre that you can't change, either.

Long spans between tyre changes can basically weld lug nuts in place. A little dab of penetrating oil – or in a pinch, a splash of something fizzy – will usually loosen rusted lug nuts quite quickly. Measure the pressure in your spare each time you check the other tyres, since long periods of inactivity can bleed the air out. Having a can of inflatable tyre sealant is always a good idea, although they make repairs more difficult at the tyre shop.

Now that you know where everything is, understand how to operate the jack, and have a functional spare tyre, you can relax. You probably won't get a flat the rest of your life. However, if you still manage to stick something pointy in one of your tyres, make sure you find a safe, level place to change your tyre. Hopefully this means a nice well-lit car park, but it's often the side of the road. If this is the case, turn on your hazard warning lights and keep your feet out of the road. Always turn off the engine and use the handbrake.

Slide the jack under the axle or jack plate next to the flat tyre, making certain it's seated firmly so it won't slip. Pry off the hubcap with the flat end of the socket bar or tyre iron, and then use the ratchet to slightly loosen each of the lug nuts, but do not remove them. Then jack up the tyre, remove the lug nuts (a hubcap works well to hold them), and slide the tyre off. Put the spare on, and then start the thread on each lug nut with your fingers. Use the ratchet to tighten each lug nut until the tyre starts to spin, then lower the jack for the final tightening.

You'll want to drive slowly at first, making sure there's no wobble in the tyre. You'll get the hang of it in no time, especially if you practice first. Soon enough you'll be able to change a tyre in five minutes.

Well... maybe ten.

Change brakes

Brakes last an average of about 20,000–40,000 miles, depending on how and where you drive. If you live in Norfolk you're likely to get more life out of your brakes than if you live in San Francisco, for instance. For some drivers, this can mean changing brakes as often as every year – an expensive proposition.

Car mechanics are, by and large, a decent bunch of people, but they're out to make a few quid like anybody else. They will overcharge you for anything even remotely complicated. The good news is changing brake pads isn't complicated, and it doesn't take much in the way of tools, either.

In almost every car, disc brakes are now the norm. The design is simple – imagine holding up a bicycle and spinning the rear wheel. You want the wheel to stop, so you press your thumb and forefinger on each side of the tyre, using friction to stop it from spinning. With disc brakes, your thumb and finger are the pads (discs); the spinning bicycle tyre is the rotor (a dinner plate-sized metal disc attached to the axle, just behind the actual car tyre). Your hand is like the calliper, which holds the pads in place and squeezes the rotor.

In many vehicles, the front brakes bear the majority of the braking duties and are consequently usually the only ones that need to be replaced. Some newer vehicles have computerized mechanisms that distribute more braking power to the rear tyres, in which case you'll probably have to replace all four sets.

So, to begin. Jack up the car and remove one of the front tyres. You'll see the calliper perched on the top half of the rotor. Most callipers are held in place by two long bolts, usually with a star- or hex-indent head, located on the backside of the rotor. Loosen and remove the two bolts, then carefully remove the calliper from the rotor – it'll slide off. Don't twist the calliper or let it drop – the brake lines could break or crimp.

Check the rotor for grooves or wear; it should be smooth. If your car was shaking when you braked, you'll need new rotors no matter how they look: the shaking is caused by a warped rotor, which can be hard to spot. Simply remove the rotor – you may need to beat on the back side with a rubber mallet or piece of wood. Worn rotors can be 'turned', which means the metal is ground smooth by a mechanic. Or, you can simply replace the warped or grooved rotors with new ones.

They slide right onto the hub. Be careful not to get any grease or dirt on the new (or repaired) rotors. Next, remove the old pads (two per calliper, one for each side of the rotor) and snap in the new brake pads. Replace pads one at a time, using the other side as a template to make sure you put them in the right way.

Use large pliers or channel locks to gently open up the inside of the callipers again – the pressure of the braking system tends to close up the pads when they're not pressing on the rotor. At this point you may have some brake fluid spill out onto the floor, so be sure to have a drain

cont.....

pan positioned under the brake fluid reservoir. Again, be careful not to get grease or oil on the pads. Slide the calliper back over the rotor.

Insert the two long bolts and retighten the calliper, then replace the tyre and retighten it. You must replace brakes on both sides of the car in one sitting; replacing only one side can cause the braking system to fail. Once all the brakes are replaced, go for a slow test drive on a level road. If you hear metal scratching you probably put the brake pads on the wrong way (yep, I've done this). Just take the tyre off and put them back in the right way – the metal tabs will score the rotor.

Pads and rotors can be bought at any car supply shop. All you need to tell the bloke behind the counter is the make and model of your vehicle, plus the year it was made. Time-wise, bank on spending an hour per tyre, maybe twice that the first time you change them. That's it. After the test drive, go out and do your bit for the national economy by celebrating the hundreds of pounds you just saved, by spending them immediately.

Fix a flat tyre

Tyres come in two basic varieties: tubed and, err, tubeless. Don't be overwhelmed by the technical language here. The difference – and this comes as a shock to some people – is the presence of an inner tube. An inner tube is a rubber bladder on the inside of the thick outer tyre. Tubeless tyres are generally harder to repair yourself, but not impossible. If there's any doubt, look on the wall of the tyre – the presence of an inner tube should be clearly marked.

Patching inner tubes: You can patch tyres' inner tubes with a simple repair kit available at most car part stores. Remove the valve core, a piece of threaded metal inside the valve stem (where you normally inflate the tyre) with valve pliers; if there's any air left in the tyre, it'll come rushing out all at once. Sometimes a pair of thin needle-nose pliers can be substituted for valve pliers.

Now slide the flat edge of a crowbar over the rim and under the inside edge of the tyre – not the inner tube. If you pinch the inner tube you've just doubled your work, as they're flimsy and puncture easily. Push the crowbar down, which will open up a gap in the tyre. Then, using either another crowbar or a large screwdriver, move down the arc of the rim and pry up another section of tyre. Working a section at a time, move down far enough with the second crowbar so that the original one doesn't slide back over the rim. Once you reach the halfway point things get a lot easier.

Once the tyre is off the rim, reach inside and slide the inner tube out. If you can't see the puncture, just add some air to the inner tube, then mark the leaky hole with a marker or grease pencil. Really small holes

cont.....

can be located by pushing the inflated tube into a trough of water and looking for bubbles.

Sand the area around the puncture with a scuffing plate or sandpaper, then apply the patch from the repair kit and clamp it into place. Burn the rubber patch on, allow it to cool, and re-inflate the tube to confirm the patch is working (you'll need to temporarily reinstall the valve core). Deflate the inner tube, and then carefully slide it back inside the tyre. Make sure you match up the valve stem with the hole in the rim.

Now, working in reverse, use the crowbars to pop the tyre back underneath the rim, again being careful not to pinch your newly repaired inner tube. Once the tyre is back over the edge of the rim, coat the edges with dish soap, then reinstall the valve stem and air it up. The tyre will expand outward, then pop when it seals. The dish soap helps lubricate the rim, helping the tyre slide up to form a bead.

Patching tubeless tyres: Tubeless tyres involve a slightly different approach. If the leak is coming from the side wall of the tyre – then the tyre is ruined. Large holes, caused by things such as jagged metal debris, will also send your tyre to the scrap heap, no matter where they are in the tyre.

Simple nail holes are a different kettle of fish. Rubber strip repair kits come with plugs, plug holders, and a pilot hole driller. Pull out the offending nail, screw or whatever caused your flat tyre. Then use the pilot hole driller – basically a sharpened file – to ream out the hole. Thread a rubber plug onto the plug holder, push the plug in at least halfway (but never all the way), then twist the plug holder and pull it out. The plug should stick in the hole and form an airtight seal.

Plugs are meant to be temporary fixes. One of my temporary fixes lasted almost thirty thousand miles, but that's because I'm a legend (only joking). Regardless, these tyre repair kits, together with a twelve-volt air compressor, can get you back on the road in minutes.

Jump-start a car

A dead battery is about the most common mechanical problem you're likely to run into. Some manufacturers recommend avoiding jump-starting newer vehicles to avoid electrical surges that could damage the computer system. Done correctly, however, a jump start won't hurt anything.

First turn off all blowers, radios, lights – anything that requires power. This applies to both the dead and the 'jumper' vehicle. Then connect the negative (black) cable from the negative post – marked with a minus (-) sign – on the dead vehicle to either the negative post, or the metal frame on the running vehicle. Then connect the positive (usually red or orange) cable from the positive post on the dead vehicle to the positive post (marked with a +) on the running vehicle. You'll hear a drop in the RPMs in the running vehicle once everything is connected properly.

Rev the engine on the jumper vehicle to increase the amount of amps flowing into the dead battery. If the battery was completely drained, you'll need to do this for a couple of minutes before the dead car will start. Larger-bore jumper cables work much faster than cheaper, thin-gauge jumper cables.

Disconnect the cables after the car starts, avoiding contact between the negative and positive clamps. While the resulting spark show is pretty cool, this could cause electrical problems to the vehicle still attached to the cables. Up to you.

Change spark plugs

One of the easiest ways to increase both mileage and horsepower is to change spark plugs and wires every 50,000 miles or so. It's also one of the most neglected maintenance jobs. No doubt mass hypnosis and an oil company executive are involved somewhere in the mix.

'Gapping' refers to setting the distance between the electrode and the plate, which will determine the length of the spark. Plug ends tend to wear down over time, and are prone to carbon build-up. While you can clean and gap old plugs, for the best performance just replace the plugs with new ones. They're only a few pounds apiece, and if you've got significant mileage on your car the plugs are probably ready for retirement anyway.

Some new spark plugs come pre-gapped, while others are adjustable. Use a simple gapping tool for the adjustable plugs, making sure the setting matches up with the manufacturer's specifications.

The easiest way to check your spark plug wires' efficiency is to open up the bonnet at night, or in a dark garage, while the car is running. Bad wires will light up the motor like twinkling Christmas lights. This is spark that should be going to your cylinders, but since the rubber sleeves crack over time, the electrical current is now arcing onto the grounded motor block. This translates into wasted power, less power, and more petrol bought at the pump each week.

You'll need one plug and one wire per cylinder. For almost every motor vehicle on the market this will be four, six, or eight. A couple of economy cars operate on three cylinders; trade this in for a real car while you're buying spark plugs. If you can't see some of the plugs, you may have to remove parts of the intake manifold to get to them during the replacement (common in some V-6s). The key is to remove one plug and one wire at a time.

On older vehicles, spark plug wires lead from the spark plug to a central hub, called a distributor, which is supplied with central current via a coil. Newer vehicles may have independent coils for each cylinder. In either case, if you don't reconnect the wires in the proper sequence you'll affect the timing, which can have some pretty disastrous consequences.

Think along the lines of those Indiana Jones movies, where Harrison Ford is weaving his way through a gallery of swinging axes and flame spurts, stopping and going at just the right time to avoid being killed. Now move old Indy forward a half-second in your mind's eye and you'll start to get the drift. Timing, as they say, is everything.

Pull the wire off the plug, then use a deep-well socket (usually around a five-eighths-inch) to unthread the plug. It's important to have a deep-well versus the standard, shallower sockets, which won't reach down low enough to grip the sides of the spark plug. Remove the plug and hand-thread the new one into place. Apply final pressure carefully. If the plug is too loose, it could blow right off; too tight and you risk breaking it off. These aren't good things, so use a torque socket or wrench to be safe.

Once you're done, fire it up and listen to the motor with a fine ear. A choppy sound indicates one or more of the cylinders are 'missing' – that is, not firing. Go back and recheck all your wire connections, making sure to push down hard on the plug ends. It should give a soft click when it's fully engaged. If the problem persists, recheck your gap settings.

Change oil and air filters

I have a confession to make. A deep and dark secret, the kind of thing no 'real man' should probably admit to. Ah sod it, it's not that bad – my wife changes my oil. Checks my air filter, too. She also irons my y-fronts and makes me a packed lunch every day but she cost me enough so I'm going to get my money's worth.

Of course, I've changed my oil and air filter many times, a simple task all blokes should know how to do – as should their wives, girlfriends, sisters, or anyone else they can talk into doing the dirty work for them. It's easy and cheap, and done regularly is about the best thing you can do to keep your car running smoothly.

You'll have to find out what kind of oil filter you need first. Ask the man in the shop, or just look under the bonnet and jot down the number on the side of the oil filter (sometimes you'll need to crawl underneath the car to find the filter). The oil cap will indicate how much and what type of motor oil you'll need. In bitterly cold climates, such as in Newcastle, switching over to a lighter grade in the winter makes good sense, since it's less viscous and reaches the pistons a little quicker on those frosty mornings.

Once you've got oil and a filter, the only other thing you need is a wrench, drain pan and maybe an oil filter wrench. Slide underneath the car (use ramps if necessary) and find the drain plug. This is usually about a quarter to a third of the way back from the front of the car, under the oil pan. The oil pan is metal, usually square with rounded edges, and the drain plug is simply a bolt head. Newer vehicles can have a plastic shroud on the underside, which makes accessing your oil pan more difficult.

Remove the drain plug and let the oil drain into a pan. If there's any doubt in your mind that this isn't the oil pan, just check the oil level after all the fluid has drained out. It should be mostly dry, with just traces of oil on the dipstick.

Next, locate the oil filter and twist it loose. If you can't do it by hand, use a filter wrench (a few quid at any automotive shop) or large channel locks. For really sticky filters, drive a screwdriver right through the oil filter and use the handle for leverage. More oil will flow out once the filter is loosened, so have the drain pan in position.

Rub some fresh oil along the rubber gasket on the new filter, then thread it on and hand tighten. Don't use a filter wrench to tighten it (or the screwdriver trick, for that matter). Unless you're very weak – perhaps from too much personal 'oil-changing' done in the privacy of your own study – hand tightening provides a perfect seal. Then thread the drain plug back into place and tighten it securely with the wrench.

Fill the car up with fresh oil, checking the dipstick occasionally so you don't overfill. Oil level should be within the two lines. Start her up, keeping an eye on the oil pressure gauge and the temperature gauge. If either one moves into the red, or if you hear any funny noises coming from your engine, immediately shut off the car and check the oil again. Starting the car will pressurize your oil system,

cont.....

and much like turning on your water mains after a plumbing repair, this is the time when you'll see if you have any leaks.

Odds are you won't. Check the oil again the next day, and again in a week to be sure everything is fine. The whole process takes about ten minutes and usually costs £10–£15. Any commercial oil-change place is obliged to take your used oil at minimal or no charge. They won't advertise it, but it's the law. Just place your used oil in a sealable vessel and drop it off. Most places will limit you to a certain quantity per visit.

Air filters are even easier to check and replace. There's usually a gauge on the outside of the air filter, a clear plastic cylinder that will say, roughly, 'change when red'. I don't really trust these gauges, and neither do many mechanics. Instead, open up the bonnet and unlatch the plastic compartment which houses the air filter, then remove the filter.

Sometimes you'll find strange material inside the air filter housing, such as dog food, straw and cigarette butts. It's not the neighbour playing tricks, just mice looking for somewhere warm to eat their cheese in peace. Vacuum all this out, and then kick that fat cat off the sofa and sling him into the garage (a clogged air filter can cause serious problems and drastically reduce mileage; the smell of cat is one of the best mouse-repellents around).

Now, hold up your air filter and shine a torch through it. The amount of light coming through the filter is a good indication of how much air can get through. If you're still not sure if it needs replacement, bang the air filter lightly against the wall. If you see a dust cloud, the air filter is probably close to saturation and needs replacing. Just purchase a new one from an auto shop and slide it into the plastic housing. They cost about £10–£20.

Rotate tyres

Tyres do not wear evenly, especially in older vehicles, when ball joints begin to wear out, causing the tyre to ride at a slight angle. There's no need to buy new tyres just because one side is more worn than the other – you just need to rotate the positions of the tyres so you have fresh rubber in the areas with the most road pressure.

Use a penny to check the depth of your treads. Slide the edge of the coin between the treads, head pointed down, and measure the amount of tread left on each side of the tyre. If you have sufficient but uneven tread then you'll want to rotate your tyres. If you can see the Queen's entire head across the tyre width, it's best to replace your tyres, since they're too worn to provide proper traction.

Jack up one tyre and remove it, then block the axle using a jack-stand or big block of wood and move to the opposite corner of the vehicle. Remember to apply the emergency brake first, and always work on a level surface. The whole process takes less than an hour, extends the length of your tyre's service, and often provides a smoother ride and even better petrol mileage.

As a side note, excessive wear on the inside (middle) of the tyre indicates a too-high air pressure; wear on both of the outside edges indicates underinflated tyres. If your front tyres have excessive wear on just one side, you may have worn front-end components, which can cause the tyre to tilt and ride slightly on edge. You'll probably want to get a mechanic to sort those out.

Fix minor dents

The easiest and most effective do-it-yourself approach to minor dents on someone else's car is to get the hell out of there as quickly and unobtrusively as possible, keeping the wife and kids from asking too many unwelcome questions.

The easiest and most effective do-it-yourself approach for minor dents on your own car is to use an auto-body filler. Sand away the paint inside the dent and an inch or two around the perimeter, then fill in the dent with body filler. Allow it to dry, then sand it smooth and prime it. Most vehicles come with a small bottle of touch-up paint, which has your vehicle's paint number on it if you need to order more.

Cover the primed area with several coats of paint, being sure to feather the edges for a natural appearance. Minor pings caused by car doors or hail can frequently be cured with a hair dryer or just prolonged exposure to the sun, especially with dark-coloured vehicles. For wide, shallow dents, try the plunger trick. Wet the end of the plunger to get better suction, then pull out steadily.

Some car shops also sell pull-type repair kits, in which you drill a small hole, then insert a spreader through the hole, expand it, and pull the dent out via a connecting cable. You can then apply putty to the hole and paint it to match the rest of the vehicle. You can always remove interior components and try to bang out the dent with a rubber mallet, but with modern vehicles it seems like you have to dismantle half the car first.

Diagnose common engine problems – and fix them

No matter what else you do, there is an essential first step to diagnosing a stalled engine. First, open up the bonnet and stare down at the engine. Then frown and shake your head slowly. Finally – and this is important – say, in a disgusted tone of voice, 'I used to understand these things, but now...' Absolutely essential. Though a downright lie.

Truth is, new engines are quite different to older models, especially since fuel injection and electronic ignition became the norm. Yet no matter how complicated they may seem, all combustion-engined vehicles still operate on the same principles as Henry Ford's first Model T, and there are usually only three possible problems with a stalled or poorly running engine: spark, fuel or air.

Before we dive into the engine stuff, first determine if you have a dead battery. If the car barely turns, or you hear a clicking noise (the solenoid) you may just need a simple jump start. You'll also want to check that both of your main battery cables are connected firmly to your battery and the negative has a firm ground. They can wiggle loose over time.

If you have battery power (the lights shine brightly, the radio still blares out Take That's *Greatest Hits*, etc) but the car won't even turn over, you may have a bad solenoid or a stuck starter. If the lights dim and you hear clicking (the solenoid) when you try to start it, tap on the starter a few times with a hammer. Starters can seize up and often just need a little persuasion to engage the flywheel.

If there isn't clicking, and the lights don't dim, try jumping the solenoid. The solenoid, either a simple relay or a cylinder about half the size of a beer can, will have two or four metal bolts, or posts, sticking out or covered by a removable plastic cap. Use a screwdriver to bridge the solenoid post to the large positive post.

Make sure the key is 'on' (full power to the accessories, without actually engaging the starter) and the car is in neutral. Jumping the solenoid provides electrical current to the starter, which turns the motor over. Use a rubber-handled screwdriver to jump the posts to avoid minor shocks – sparks will fly. Except for the lack of a handy remote control, this is also how those nifty remote car starters work. Solenoids can be on the starter, as shown, or situated somewhere along the firewall. Finding the solenoid is often the major challenge.

If the car turns over but still won't start, you've eliminated both a dead battery and a bad solenoid. This narrows the problem down to the same three elements needed for any fire: air, fuel and spark. Of these three, air is the least likely to cause trouble. However, a disconnected vacuum hose can prevent the engine from starting, so look for any obviously disconnected hoses. A plugged air filter can also prevent a car from running.

Once you've eliminated air problems, check for spark. The easiest way to do this is to disconnect a spark plug, then reattach the plug wire and ground the plug to a bare metal surface. Either hold the plug against bare metal, or use a screwdriver as a bridge. Get a friend to turn the engine over – you should see a spark jump between the

cont.....

electrode and the plate. If not, you've just diagnosed a spark problem. Leave the spark plug out for diagnostic purposes. And use those exact words if someone asks what you're doing.

One of the most common causes of a spark problem is moisture. If it's raining, or if you just drove through a large puddle, you'll want to check your distributor for moisture. This is the central hub for your spark (in older vehicles) and often collects moisture. Take off the distributor cap and wipe it dry with your T-shirt, then try to start your engine. Newer vehicles probably won't have a distributor.

If you still don't have spark, try spraying a light oil lubricant like WD-40 over the spark plug wires. This will displace any water inside the sheathing, and is sometimes all you need to get sufficient spark into your cylinders. If you still don't have spark, your coil(s) might be cracked and collecting moisture. Use a hair dryer to dry it out (newer vehicles might have a coil attached for each plug).

The most common fuel problems involve the fuel pump and filter. A clogged fuel filter is easily diagnosed, since it results in a gradual loss of power over time, and is easy to replace. Follow the fuel line forward from the petrol tank until you see the filter, usually about the size of a drinks can. Unscrew the fuel line on each end, then insert the new one and refasten it, making sure the arrow is pointing from the tank toward the engine. You'll get some petrol on your hands, so hold off on that celebratory fag until you wash up.

A bad fuel pump is more likely to strand you somewhere. While a bad fuel pump can be diagnosed by the presence of a jumpy or non-responsive fuel gauge, or a long turnover before the engine starts, sometimes they stop working with no warning at all. To check if your fuel pump is working, turn the key forward, without actually starting the engine; you should hear a faint buzzing from the fuel tank. If not, you might have a bad fuel pump. In all likelihood, you'll need a mechanic to replace it. This is the bad news.

Now, if your fuel pump goes out while you're driving, you're just plain-old buggered. That's all there is to it. There's no easy fix, no way to get it started; just tow it to the mechanic and fork out the money. But to avoid pick up-truck expense, pay attention to any shaking in your fuel gauge. Coupled with problems starting your vehicle beforehand, or significant mileage, it's a good sign your fuel pump is about to go. Make an appointment with a mechanic before you get stranded somewhere.

The good news is a faulty fuel pump can sometimes be fixed, but only if it gave up working when the engine was off. Fuel pumps can get stuck, locked into place as the components begin to break down, but you can often jar that old fuel pump into action one more time. The secret? Bang on the bottom of the fuel tank. Bang on it with a hammer, piece of wood, or even your fist. While this might jar the fuel pump loose, it only works once. If it starts, drive it straight to the repair garage.

Still no luck? Much of your vehicle operates electronically, and all electrical functions are controlled by fuses. Many vehicles have two sets of fuses, one for smaller functions like windscreen wipers and interior lighting (usually located in the interior, in the glove box or under the steering wheel) and another for heavier-duty stuff, like fuel pumps, which are usually located under the bonnet. It's worth a look; bad fuses will have a burned-out metal strip in the centre. Replace any burned out fuses with a less critical one until you can buy a new one.

Getting yourself unstuck

Sometimes having four-wheel drive can be a mixed blessing. It's extremely useful for getting out of tough spots (like the yummy-mummy scrum outside the local prep school of a morning), but it also gets you into spots you have no right to be in the first place (see above). And that, invariably, is when it stops working.

Let's assume this particular prep school is at the bottom of a waterlogged dirt track somewhere in rural Chelsea. Don't spin your tyres once it's obvious you're stuck; this is what psychologists call your denial phase. The only exception to this rule is if you have someone you don't care for standing behind you – a stuck vehicle can throw up an awesome amount of mud.

If you can move a little, creep in one direction until your tyres begin to slip. Then stop, reverse directions, and go back until the tyres spin again. Keep rocking the car back and forth, with the front tyres straight, and try to extend the 'stuck lane' until you can build up enough momentum to break free.

If you can't move at all, take out your car jack and raise the power tyre (the one that's spinning). You may need to put something solid under the jack if you're in soft mud – a thick tree limb or even your spare tyre works in a pinch. Once the tyre is off the ground, put some roughage under it for traction. Tree boughs or foliage provide excellent traction and are fairly common, but sticks, or gravel from the shoulder of the road, will also work. You may want to line the rut you're in with branches or sticks so you don't get stuck as soon as you leave your original rut. If at first you don't succeed, try again. And make sure you do actually have four-wheel drive engaged if you have it.

Hook up a trailer

An old friend of mine absolutely loved to fish off his own boat. In fact, he was so anxious to get on the water that he often rushed off without double-checking his tackle, and would frequently arrive at the lake minus some important piece of gear. On a trip many years ago, he forgot about the most important thing you can bring on a fishing trip.

Well, no, he did remember the beer. Second most important thing, then – his boat. That's right. He travelled over 50 miles in his estate packed to the gunwales, his rear view blocked, before he realized his trailer had come loose and his boat trailer had slid free on the motorway, at 60 miles an hour, somewhere just past the Scottish border. I can't imagine the feeling he had when he pulled off the road, got out to stretch, and saw the empty space behind his car. Knowing him, I can imagine the words that came out of his mouth. My ears ring just thinking about it.

Unbelievably, he found his boat and trailer sitting by the side of the road, unscathed, just a couple of hours later. He was pretty lucky, though (to qualify as really lucky he wouldn't have had any witnesses), because a trailer coming loose can cause serious injury to the trailer, its load, and anybody following you.

First, check to make sure you have the right size ball hitch for the trailer you're going to haul. Most hitches are made for 2-inch balls, but there are still quite a few 1 ⅞-inch ball hitches and receivers around.

Look on the top of the ball; there should be a size etched into the metal. There should also be a size etched into the top of the coupler

cont.....

handle. Basically – fundamentally – these have to match up. Ideally, your ball hitch should be attached to a ball mount, which slides into a receiving hitch, which in turn is bolted right to the frame of your vehicle. Bumper-mounted ball hitches are too high for heavy loads, resulting in an angled trailer, and form a weak connection to the frame.

Now, slide the coupler down and over the ball. If it sticks, make sure the trailer is lined up straight. Then bring the coupler handle down, and slide a bolt or pin through the hole. Otherwise, all it takes is one good bump and the handle can pop up. One more bump and the coupler could bounce off the ball, and you're suddenly at a fishing lake without a bloody boat.

Cross the safety chains for the best holding power. Attach them to the frame, not the bumper; most receiver hitches have a couple of holes to the side of the ball mount to attach the safety chains. Leave enough slack in the chains so you can make wide turns without them coming tight, yet not so much slack that the chains drag on the ground. As a final safety precaution, some trailers come equipped with an emergency brake, which is activated by a trip lever attached to a thin metal cable. Again, attach this cable somewhere to the frame. If both the trailer coupler and the safety chains come loose, the cable will engage the emergency brake and stop the trailer.

Now you need some lights. Simply slide the light adaptor for the trailer into the wiring harness on your towing vehicle. Sometimes this is flat and rectangular, commonly called a flat four. Flat fours have been largely replaced with circular, plug-style wiring connectors. If you have the wrong type of wiring connection, you can buy a conversion kit and install it in a few minutes. The older type of connector is prone to corrosion, but a shot of WD-40 and a small wire brush can cure any contact issues in short order.

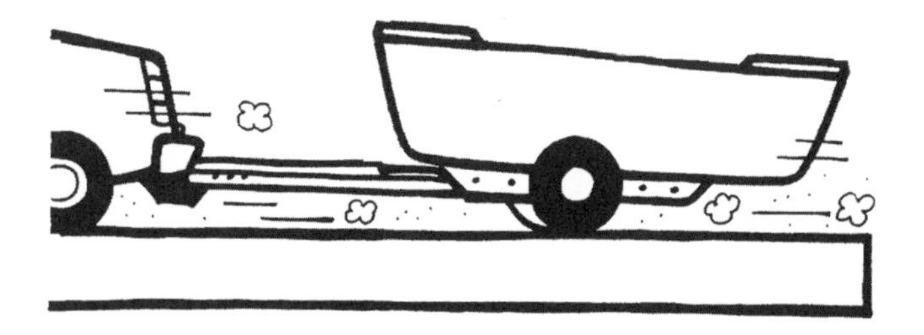

Reverse a trailer

One of the easiest tricks in the world when it comes to backing up a trailer? Straighten the vehicle and trailer so they're in line, then put your right hand on the bottom of the steering wheel, at the six o'clock position. Now slowly begin to reverse. No trailer will move perfectly straight no matter how good you are; reversing a trailer involves constant minute adjustments that are best made at a slow speed.

Looking in the rear-view or wing mirrors, rotate your steering-wheel hand in the direction you want the trailer to go. If you want it to go left, bring the hand gripping the steering wheel up in that direction. If you want it to go right, swing your hand back in that direction. This one-handed approach eliminates the mental confusion associated with interpreting a reflected object, and allows you to sit comfortably, instead of twisting your body around.

If you're backing up an empty trailer and can't see the sides of the trailer, drop the tailgate of your pickup or open the rear door of your SUV. Again, just move slowly and make minor adjustments as you back up.

A few extra tips:

1. If you're backing a boat trailer into the water, be sure you disconnect the wiring before submerging the lights. Submerging your trailer lights is an easy way to blow out either a bulb or a fuse.
2. The shorter the trailer tongue, the tougher it is to back up the trailer. Go slower to make up for the lower margin of error.
3. Never leave your vehicle unattended while parked on a ramp. If you have to load the boat alone, set the emergency brake and use chocks under the tyres.
4. If you're pulling a trailer in an automatic vehicle, use the next lowest gear. There's no need to use third or second gear just because you're pulling a trailer; just make sure the transmission isn't being overtaxed by excessive shifting.

Ride a motorbike

My wife is always scared my bike is going to get me killed. I tell her it won't be my bike that kills me, it'll be the front bumper of an HGV on the wrong side of the road that'll pack me off. But so far, the thing I've hurt the most has been my pride.

I've killed the engine at busy junctions, been hit with a rock in the very worst place a man can get hit at 70 miles an hour (no, not in the eye), slid under a car and burned my leg so badly on the muffler that my skin turned into patches of greenish-purple bubbles, and wiped out after getting unseated by a bird. Yes, a bird. Motorbikes are dangerous, no doubt about it. Of course, they're also about as much fun as you can have on your own in public without a disguise.

If you're familiar with driving a manual car, you're well on your way to learning to drive a motorcycle. The main difference is that a motorcycle uses a hand-operated clutch and throttle, with a foot-operated gear shifter. Braking is applied via both hand and foot, but only on the right side of the vehicle. Don't worry, it's not nearly as complicated as it sounds.

To start, you'll want the bike in neutral with the handbrake applied. Reach down and flip open the kickstart (or, if you want to be a pansy, use the electronic start). Once it fires up, press in the hand-clutch, and press the foot lever down. For most bikes, only the first gear is down, with the rest being up. You should hear a click as the foot lever pops up, which means you're in first gear. Let the hand clutch out, applying throttle. Continue shifting up on the foot lever until you reach top gear (usually fifth) and then downshift by pressing down on the clutch pedal until you reach neutral.

You can't steer a motorcycle much by moving the handlebars, unless you're going under ten miles per hour. Instead, steering a bike is accomplished by leaning, exerting slight pressure on one side of the handlebars while shifting your body weight into the curve. Start out slow, making both wide and tight curves, before heading out onto the main roads. Be careful not to overcompensate, and don't take passengers right away, since they make steering much more difficult.

Unlike a car, the front and back brakes are separated. Many people brake almost exclusively with the rear brake, which makes steering during the slowdown easier, and also prevents the front tyre from 'ploughing', or suddenly turning sideways and dumping you into the road. Hard braking with the rear tyre, however, can cause the back tyre to slide out from underneath you on loose gravel or wet roads. I generally apply about 75 per cent braking to the rear and 25 per cent to the front, but the exact ratio depends on road conditions and on the kind of bike you drive.

Your headlights should stay on all the time. Most accidents happen because motorcycles are tough to see and people pull out in front of them, so it's imperative you watch for inattentive drivers. Also watch for deer, dogs (they love to chase motorcycles, the mangy little bastards), and yes, even birds. Wear a helmet and shades. Bright clothing is recommended, so maybe this is your chance to break out that lime green, tie-dyed T-shirt.

cont.....

The key is to practice at slow speeds, which are the safest if you happen to wipe out, and also the hardest to master. High speed steering is easy, as long as you don't overcompensate on a curve or hit something. So go on out there and join the club. It doesn't matter what you drive. Riding a bike is like being part of a gang, even if you don't smash up backwater bars and chase pills with Jim Beam for breakfast. No matter what you drive, nine times out of ten you'll get a little wave from another biker when you meet on the road; if you run into trouble, the first bloke there is probably going to roll to a stop on two wheels. We stick together, because when you get hit by a fat insect in the lip at 70 miles an hour, everyone bleeds the same colour. Well, except for the insects – they bleed a sort of yellowish-green.

THE SPORTING LIFE

Hit a straight drive

Some blokes are natural golfers. I'm a natural slicer, prone to big swings and what one friend refers to as 'that unique flying elbow'. Occasionally I try to play my slice by teeing up toward the woods, in the vague hope my ball will curve back onto the fairway. This is invariably when I hit my straightest drives, the ones where the ball screams out at a perfect trajectory, rising high off the ground until it thunks into a poplar tree a hundred yards away.

Ironically, inconsistency is consistently the single biggest problem facing the average weekend golfer, and the only thing that can cure inconsistency is practice – lots and lots of practice. Since most of us just don't have the time to hit ten buckets of balls each week, we'll concentrate on some minor adjustments that can straighten out many of those errant drives.

Slices and hooks are caused by spin, which results from the clubface hitting the ball at an angle. Spin is inevitable, of course, but the key to straight drives is reducing sidespin by presenting a straight clubface to the ball. Easier said than done, but there are a couple of tricks that can help significantly reduce the sidespin that causes slices and hooks.

First, try adjusting the height of the tee so you're only about half an inch off the ground. Many people tee up much too high, which affects the point in your swing at which you make contact. Since the very bottom of your swing is the point at which the clubface is the most stable, simply pushing the tee down an extra half-inch to extend your arms a little more can drastically reduce sidespin.

Another old trick, passed on to me by my father-in-law, seems to work wonders for some people. Stick a handkerchief under the armpit closest to the pin, then simply make your swing without letting the handkerchief fall to the ground. Done correctly, this eliminates that flying elbow, presents a straighter clubface to the ball, and makes for straighter drives (and yeah, maybe a few funny looks).

Hit the ball toward the inside part of the clubface, which has less wiggle than the outside edge. Keep your eye on the ball, letting your momentum carry your head upward. Looking up before you hit the ball shifts your entire stance, which in turn shifts the clubface.

Lastly, and perhaps most importantly, try taking about ten per cent off the force of your swing. Any more than this and your grip tends to suffer, resulting in a floppy swing and weak, dribbling drives. But backing off ten per cent can work wonders, relaxing your muscles just enough to give a smooth yet still powerful swing.

Odds are you aren't going to be making the next European Masters tour even if you follow these little bits of advice. But you might stay on the green a few more times each round, and that's all most of us want anyway. If not, well... the woods are nice and shady on those hot summer days.

Get out of a bunker

Hitler, Saddam Hussein, Colonel Gaddafi. What did they all have in common? Yes, that's right – they were all keen golfers in their day, and also had a great affinity with bunkers.

Anyway, to get out of one made of sand... first, make sure nobody's looking. Usually this is right after someone who's a lot better than you bounces their ball onto the green. Then, while everyone's attention is diverted, grab your ball and lob it, quickly followed by a swing into the sand and a victorious/relieved whoop.

You'll want to be consistent with your previous results; depending on how you're playing, you can either throw it onto the green or merely out of the trap. To keep everybody fooled, I usually throw mine into the woods.

A couple of less efficient but more ethical options involve the scoop and the plough techniques. Quite simply, you can either: 1. Try to pluck the ball out of the sand, assuming it isn't buried in the stuff and instead is just sitting there, looking like it's going to be the easiest shot you've had this whole miserable round, or 2. Hit just behind the ball, using the resulting explosion of sand to lift the ball up and out of the trap.

Both methods work. The scoop method involves a normal swing, but it requires a nearly perfect hit. Try moving back when addressing the ball, which means you'll catch the ball on your upswing and get better lift. A smooth follow-through and pinpoint accuracy are essential when using this technique, so take lots of practice swings.

The plough method seems simpler, yet is often more difficult for the average golfer. Basically, you're trying to create a small tidal wave of sand underneath the ball, which will lift it up and out of the trap. You'll have to hit the sand pretty hard to do this, and you need to hit right behind the ball – if you connect with the ball you're going to end up sailing way over the green and into the clubhouse. When this does work, however, the results are pretty good.

I still opt for the hand toss. Does that make me a tosser? Yes, I suppose it does. So what – eat my bogey!

Hit out of the rough

Swing like hell. Actually, my preferred method involves using half a dozen practice swings to clear out a lane just behind the ball, then use that path of beaten-down grass as an approach lane to my buried ball. Another nice method is to feign practice swings, all the while trying to hit the ball. The trick here is to not act surprised when you actually hit the ball, and never make the mistake of wiggling the club head or – God forbid – staring down the pin. Just keep swinging, taking a small break to shuffle your feet between each swing. When the ball finally comes free, nonchalantly drop your iron back in the bag. Whatever else you do, do not look up to see your partners' expressions.

If you're one of those puritanical golf types, my first advice stands. Swing like hell, and make sure you follow through to power through the thick stuff. You'll want to open up your clubface, as the grass tends to pull the clubface in when you drag it through the rough.

If you inch a bit closer to the ball, you'll reduce the amount of grass you hit. This will also reduce backspin, so the ball will bounce longer than it might for a conventional fairway shot. The perfect shot out of the rough is going to be fairly flat, a roller more than a bouncer, so keep that in mind when selecting your club.

Greens etiquette

You tee up and, miracle of miracles, the drive goes straight and far. There's still a 100 yards to go, though, and you manage to wipe everything else out of your mind as you pull the iron out of the bag and separate from your foursome. Two practice swings, then you address the ball and everything is gone; next week's deadline, the dentist visit you've been putting off for two months in the hope the pain will just go away, the leaky sink, the stranded four-by-four – everything. Just you and the ball and the club, and there it goes, arcing into the air on a beautiful parabola, hitting the far side of the green and rolling to a stop not ten feet away from the pin.

Heaven, right? Well, depends on who you're playing with.

Time to seal the deal. At this point, concentration reaches a critical phase, with the focus centred on how the golf ball will 'play' – how it will roll according to the terrain of the green. Whether you take golf seriously or not, this isn't the time for distractions. Even normally laidback people get highly irritated with buffoonery at this point. And like all high-pressure situations, putting brings out the best and worst in people.

Listen, greens etiquette is simple. Just imagine you're playing for a hundred quid a hole, and the bloke putting is your partner. In other words, shut up and stand still until he's done. That's really all you need to remember. If you follow the rest of these simple rules, you'll be fine no matter who you golf with.

cont.....

1. The bloke farthest out goes first. If you're closer to the pin and your ball is even remotely in the way of the bloke putting behind you, place a ball marker behind your ball (a coin is fine) and pick up your ball until he's putted past you. Then set the ball down in front of the marker, pick the marker up, and make your putt.
2. Never walk between another person's ball and the hole. This can leave a depression in the green, which can alter the course of a putted ball. Walk on the outside of the balls if you need to go somewhere. Of course, never drive a mechanized cart on the green, and leave your golf bag outside the fringe.
3. Don't remove anything or alter the terrain in front of you in any way, shape or form. This includes leaves, twigs, dead badgers, etc.
4. When someone is putting, you should not be on the other side of the hole, walking, talking, dialling a number on your mobile phone, scratching your backside, or breathing heavily down the back of their neck. Just shut up and watch the clouds drift by for a few seconds.
5. If it's a long putt and the putter can't see the hole, offer to pull the flag. This means you stand next to the hole with one hand on the pole. Once the putter makes contact with the ball, pick up the flag and walk out of the way. Avoid the temptation to stop the ball with the side of your foot when it rolls past the hole. Even if the bloke putting is your boss.
6. Put the flag back up for the next group. Nothing is more distracting than running down to put up the flag before your approach shot.

Keep score in bowling

With the advent of electronic scorecards, the simple act of calculating your own bowling score is becoming a lost art. And frankly, when you're at a bowling alley surrounded by screaming kids, arcade machines at top volume and prowling hoodies high on chicken-in-a-basket and Carling top, who cares? But in order to truly understand how spares and strikes affect your final score, it's imperative you understand the basic methodology behind scoring frames. Otherwise you're playing blind.

You get two chances at each set of pins. If you knock down all the pins with your first ball, that strike, marked by an X, means you can add the next two ball totals to that score of ten. So, if you get two more strikes, your first box score will be a 30. A spare means that you use both balls to knock down ten pins. Even if you throw a gutter ball the first time and knock down all ten pins with your second ball, it's still considered a spare. If you bowl a spare, add the next ball's total to that score.

In essence, throwing a spare or strike means you can double or triple your actual score. A perfect run of strikes equals a 300 score (the tenth frame actually allows you to throw three balls, since throwing a strike in the tenth score box means you need two more ball totals to calculate the final score; if you don't get a strike or a spare, you don't get to throw the third ball in the last frame). Throwing spares consistently, along with a couple of strikes, should land you in the 150–200 score range. Not exactly Kingpin, but pretty healthy.

Bowl accurately

It was Valentine's Day, and being the romantic fool that I am, I escorted my future wife to the bowling alley. Yeah, there's nothing like the smell of lagery carpets and communal shoes to really warm the heart of your girl on a cold February afternoon.

My brother-in-law watched me warm up, arms crossed, an expression closely resembling pity etched on his face. Finally he approached and pointed to the small arrows a few feet in front of the throw line. 'Concentrate on those,' he told me. 'Don't even look at the pins.' 'Oh yeah?' 'Yep,' he said. 'They match up with the pins. That centre arrow is in line with the lead pin. The other ones correspond with side pins. Aim somewhere between the middle dot and the one alongside it.' Suddenly, as though someone had turned a switch, I could bowl.

Spares and strikes piled up on my scorecard, escalating my scores into unheard-of ranges (triple digits!). I quickly learned to throw the ball slightly off centre, hitting between the lead pin and the number-three pin behind it. I didn't throw hooks, or throw hard. I just threw straight balls, at a medium strength, concentrating on the little arrows. And man oh man, how the pins fell down.

This is easy, I remember thinking as I tallied up my score, somewhere in the 220 range. Visions of 300 games raced through my head; with a little luck, I could be wearing plaid trousers and carrying around a pro card come next Valentine's Day.

As it turns out, that game was a fluke – I haven't come close to that score since. But my game has gotten a lot better, and even throwing straight balls I can still manage a respectable score most nights. And almost all of that is because I quit looking at the pins and started looking at the arrows.

Of course, using the arrows (or dots) as a reference won't help if the ball isn't thrown on a straight line from your hand. Start out by holding the ball in both hands, slightly to the left of the arrow you have your eye on. Keep your arm loose, which allows the weight of the ball to keep your delivery arm straight. When you bring the ball forward your arm should swing loosely, like a pendulum.

Unless you're a hard-core bowler, consistent strikes are tough with a straight ball. Better to concentrate on hitting spares as often as you can and let the strikes fall when they want to. To get a good number of spares, you'll need to consistently knock down seven or more pins with your first ball.

A three-step approach will usually build up enough momentum for consistently high pin knockdowns. Start with your right foot forward; this is simply a momentum builder and can be extended back two steps if you want a five-step approach. There are lines of dots behind the foul line to show starting points for both approaches; take a couple of practice strides before you actually throw the ball. Open up your hips to let the ball pass on a straight line. The ball should leave your hand just before it makes contact with the alley. Make sure you keep your wrist straight.

Don't even look up when you release the ball; instead, see if the ball crosses the arrow you aimed for. If it crosses the correct arrow, and the ball still doesn't strike the pins where it should, there's a hitch in your delivery. Try using a heavier ball; the weight keeps your arm straighter.

Oh, and one more thing. If you find a girl who doesn't mind a greasy family bucket and cheap beer on Valentine's Day, marry her. Besides the obvious good character traits inherent with such women, they're also a guaranteed cheap date for years to come.

Throw a hook

The reason professional bowlers maintain such a high average is simple: they use a hook ball to consistently score strikes. Scientific studies have shown that an angling ball will produce more knockdown power than a straight ball, even when they hit the exact same spot, but all the proof you need is right there on the American PBA tour. It's hard to argue with a bloke who considers eight strikes per game a dismal failure.

So why doesn't everybody throw a hook? Well, it can take some time to learn. Professional bowlers split their time three ways: drinking beer, searching the Sunday ads for polyester slacks sales, and practicing their hooks (I'm kidding, of course – polyester slacks are always on sale).

They've taken years to master what looks like a very simple technique. And at its heart, throwing a hook isn't terribly difficult. Throwing a hook accurately is where the years of practice come in, for which there is no easy shortcut. Still, you should be able to throw a hook, even if it's just because it looks cool.

Nearly all league and professional bowlers use a special resin ball that produces more spin. Much like a curving free kick in football, more spin equals more movement. If you're going to use a house ball, it's usually best to stick with a light one. It takes considerable wrist strength to throw a big hook, and even powerful men who aren't regular bowlers have difficulty getting enough twist on heavy, non-resin balls.

The thumb goes in the hole, but the rest of your fingers cradle the ball from underneath. Don't tuck your little finger in, as this affects control and lessens spin. Your thumb, pointed up at one o'clock, should rotate to ten or eleven o'clock on release. Your palm should end up like you're about to shake someone's hand. Throw at a slight angle toward the right gutter; the ball should reverse movement about halfway down the alley.

Lanes are oiled to prevent damage, and this oil moves over the course of the game, spreading and thinning in some areas, piling up in others. Sometimes only the middle area is oiled, leaving the outer lanes dry. This means that each lane you play may affect the hook of your ball, so you'll need to adjust your technique according to the conditions of each bowling lane.

Pick out a decent cue

When it comes to pool cues, most people who take the game seriously use their own. Most of the rest of us, who don't take it seriously but who play occasionally at the bar or in someone else's games room, rely on a house cue of very doubtful provenance. Approximately 99.8 per cent of all house cues are as warped as your standard Jerry Springer guest, and a warped cue equals missed shots. The real trick here is to find the best of a bad lot.

To determine warp, lay the cue flat on the table and give it a little roll. Warped sticks will bounce and thump along the baize. Straight cues will roll smoothly. Now rub your finger over the tip. Smooth, hard tips don't produce much in the way of spin. There are abrasion pads made specifically for roughing up cue tips; they resemble a chalk box with an interior that feels like coarse sandpaper. If you can't find a 'scuffer' you can try to use a file or some other rough surface to soften up the tip. A soft, well-chalked tip will drastically reduce those glancing shots that are the hallmark of the amateur pool player.

Most cues will have a number written on the side, about halfway down. This is the weight of the cue in ounces, and typically ranges from the teens into the low twenties. I've always felt that heavier cues, around twenty ounces, give a smoother delivery. Some people use a heavier stick for breaking, then use a lighter one for the remainder of the game. Once you've got the stick picked out, apply chalk to the tip about every other shot. Keep your pint in your power hand, since condensation on your guide hand can cause the cue to drag during delivery.

Rack and play pool

EIGHT-BALL (STANDARD)

Start with any ball in the front, except the eight ball. Then work your way up one side of the triangle, alternating solid with striped. The eight ball goes in the middle. The two balls behind the eight can be either stripes or solids. What matters is that the outside perimeter alternates between solid and striped.

This is the racking pattern used in the vast majority of bars and games rooms across the world, although official pool rules require only the eight ball in the middle and alternating balls at the back corner. This won't be an issue unless you're playing against a snob. In this case, you can use either the standard or official pattern – depends on who's holding the bigger stick at the time.

Roll the racked balls forward until the front ball is centred on the rack mark. If you place the rack too far forward, even an inch, the breaking pattern will be disrupted, resulting in fewer balls potted on break. Most experienced pool players know this, and they won't like it.

Roll the rack back and forth a few times, position the lead ball directly over the mark, and then centre the rack so the back edge is parallel with the back rail. Now, holding the rack in place with your thumbs and little fingers, slide your index and middle fingers from both hands behind the back row of balls. This packs the balls together, resulting in what's called a tight rack.

cont.....

This increases breaking power, which makes for a cleaner, faster game. When the balls are set, carefully slide the rack up. Sometimes the lead ball will roll forward slightly when you remove the rack. If this happens, just re-rack the balls, centre and position the rack again, and then tap the lead ball with the cue ball or a ball from the back of the rack. This will stop that maddening forward roll.

NINE-BALL

Nine-ball uses a diamond-shaped rack. The nine ball is in the middle, and the one ball is in the front of the diamond. Alternate spots and stripes as you would for an eight-ball rack.

Nine-ball is played as a numerically sequential game. Simply, that means that you must pot the balls in order, from lowest to highest. One ball first, then the two, and so on. This is why the one ball has to be in front of the rack – it has to be the first ball the breaker hits. Some versions allow using combinations, such as a one ball into a nine ball for an instant win, others don't. Just ask your opponent if you're not sure. If you want to play nine-ball and don't have a nine-ball rack, you can use a triangular eight-ball rack and simply press the back half of the diamond into place with your hands. It's a fun game.

CUTTHROAT

Cutthroat pool is great if you have an uneven number of players, such as three or five, though you can play it with any number. You split teams up, then draw for your ball numbers. Keep your numbers secret. If you're playing with three people, one person would get balls one to five, another six to ten, and the last eleven to fifteen. You'll want to pot everybody else's balls and leave yours on the table – that's all there is to it. If you have an even number of people, the undrawn balls are dummies that anyone can hit in. Rack it the same as you would for eight-ball, except the eight ball doesn't have to be in the middle.

Put spin on the cue ball

I vividly remember watching my dad playing pool in the little country tavern when I was a kid. He was a fine shot in the traditional sense, but what I remember the most was how he could curve the cue ball around one ball to hit another behind it, almost as though the cue ball were on a string. It's the kind of stuff you usually only see with trick shots on satellite telly sports channels nowadays, but the use of controlled spin is an essential part of any pool player's arsenal.

Spin is primarily used to position your cue ball for a follow-up shot, or to avoid scratches. By striking the cue ball at different positions you can make it stop, roll forward, go to either side, or even reverse directions. Done correctly, this means you can position the cue ball in a spot that gives you an excellent chance at sinking another ball. Most good pool players plan at least two or three shots in advance; professionals can look at a table after the break and see all eight shots they need for a win.

The first step toward using spin is conditioning the cue tip. Scuff it thoroughly and chalk the bejesus out of it. Applying spin with a smooth, hard tip is nearly impossible.

The most common way to use spin is to make the cue ball stop dead when it makes contact with the game ball. This is very useful when the game ball is near the pocket and you have a straight-on shot, since hitting the cue ball with a normal stroke will cause you to scratch. To stop the cue ball on contact, simply hit it crisply about two-thirds of the way down.

To get backspin, hit it the same way described above, but angle the back of the stick slightly up and punch the tip through the ball – don't stop the stick once you make the initial contact. This works best on close shots, since backspin usually slows or disappears completely after the cue ball travels a couple of feet across the felt.

For topspin, hit the cue ball high, about a third of the way down, and follow through with an exaggerated motion. This is an underutilized technique for getting the cue ball out of a crammed area, or even breaking up a clump of balls after your shot. For right spin, hit the ball on the right side, and vice versa for left. A cue ball with side spin will rarely move at right angles, but instead will move diagonally upon hitting the game ball. Again, punch the cue tip through the ball with an exaggerated follow-through.

Spin is also useful for hitting the cue ball off the rail for bank shots. By putting side spin on the cue ball, you can get it to change angles when it touches the rail.

The perfect basketball jump shot

To shoot well in a game, you need to practice game-type shots. That means jumping as high as you can while maintaining some semblance of form and accuracy; it also means dribbling with your back to the hoop and quickly spinning to address the rim and shoot. Time after time after time. Lazy, unpressured practice shots don't help when it comes to nailing it during a game.

For a right-handed shooter, the left hand is a guide. Position your palm flat along the left side of the ball. Rest the fingertips of your right hand across the lacing, so your fingertips are nestled in a groove. Push forward with your right hand, angle your wrist back, then snap it forward so the ball rolls off the end of your fingers. Never push the ball straight out using your palm, no matter how hurried you are. It's very ugly and it's very inaccurate.

It's essential that your right elbow is tucked in, not cocked out to the side. You might even try aiming with your elbow – it can drastically improve accuracy if you normally shoot with a cocked elbow. In fact, keep everything in a straight line, from your toes to the tips of your outstretched fingers. If you develop a shooting style that's in-line and smooth, all you have to do is square up to the rim and judge distance. That's still quite a bit to do with a face full of defender, but it does eliminate the errors inherent with unorthodox deliveries.

A lot of your shooting range comes from your legs, not your arms. If you doubt this, stand on the three-point line and try to sink a basket without moving your feet. Since you rely on the power of your legs to power much of your shot, it's important to practice while jumping at game-level height, as mentioned earlier. Some people even put up a stepladder or other obstacle to shoot over.

Keep the ball at chest level when you start your shot. This gives you a quicker release and gets the ball up and away from the defender much faster. Release the ball at the apex of your jump, being sure to follow through with your wrist to create that all-important spin off your fingertips.

Arm-wrestle a stronger opponent

You don't have to be stronger than your opponent to beat him at arm wrestling. You can't be a lot weaker, of course – let's not descend into Revenge of the Nerds territory. You'll need to be within about 25 per cent of your opponent's upper body strength to have a chance at winning, though not necessarily their arm strength. A lot of arm-wrestling power is rooted in hand, wrist and shoulder musculature. The results are also heavily dependent on technique, and the technique you'll use depends on the relative strengths of you and your opponent.

There are a couple of ways to work out strength beforehand. Shake hands to get a feel for your opponent's hand strength, and take a quick look at his forearms and biceps to get an indication of general arm strength. Don't worry too much about his upper arm. While it certainly makes things tougher, an opponent with big biceps isn't the kiss of death. Now you'll need to come to grips with your opponent at the table.

This is no time for a weak grip; many arm-wrestling matches get bogged down in virtual stalemates, so having a psychological edge is important. This means acting like you're just getting warmed up at any point during the match, even if you've just popped a couple of veins and are trying desperately not to cry. It also means squeezing the wotsits out of your opponent's hand.

Circle your non-wrestling thumb and index finger around your opponent's elbow. He should do the same (assuming you aren't at an arm-wrestling table). This locks your elbows in place, preventing them from sliding. Don't let your opponent lift up your elbow, since this will result in a tremendous loss of power on your side; you're basically a lever without a fulcrum as soon as your elbow leaves the table.

You'll usually have a referee, who if he knows what he's doing and isn't just your retarded mate Dave, will place his hands over your combined grip. When he lets go the match begins, and the match is almost always won in the first five to ten seconds. Even if it actually goes on for a quarter-hour, both people are pretty sure how things are going to turn out within those first crucial moments. Hit your opponent with everything you have as soon as you can, since it's much harder to work uphill once you get down.

There are three basic techniques, depending on whether you feel you're stronger or weaker than your opponent.

THE HOOK

This is the standard arm-wrestling strategy used by most non-diehards. The technique is simple, but there are some subtle intricacies that can greatly improve your record. Use a hook with an opponent you feel is the same strength, or weaker, than you.

The very first thing you need to establish is hand-angle dominance. In simpler words, force your opponent's hand back and expose his wrist. Once his wrist is back, he's forced to use a different set of muscles to push against your arm pressure. To understand this better, grab your forearm just below the elbow, then make a fist and bend your wrist back and forth. You can feel the muscles shift according to your wrist position. Your stronger muscles are in the bottom part of your forearm, which is why using the hook technique is so important.

Try to pull your opponent's hand toward you. This is called backpressure, and it helps tremendously, maybe more than any other single technique.

cont.....

A straight arm exerts more pressure, which is why arm-wrestling short-armed people is tough; they inherently have a more vertical stance. But you can pull them towards you to counter their natural advantage, which will stretch their arm out and weaken their leverage.

THE TOPROLL

The toproll is a fairly advanced technique that allows you to beat stronger opponents. It's best to practice the grip movement and application of backpressure beforehand, so it doesn't seem like a rehearsed move.

Besides, you'll need to quickly perform the toproll before your stronger opponent slams your arm down. The key is to work your hand up your opponent's grip by walking your fingers up through your opponent's palm. Done successfully, your hand will wrap around the top part of his hand and he'll be stuck holding your wrist or the bottom part of your hand. Apply as much backpressure as possible, and you can beat pretty much anybody in the place (in your approximate strength range). Both the hook and the toproll benefit greatly from a third technique, which is actually more of a finishing move, called the press.

THE PRESS

This involves rotating your body so that your shoulder and body weight are in line with the direction you want your arm to go.

Unless your opponent is extremely strong, he'll be unable to move your whole body unless he rotates against you. Easy enough, but many people take the term arm-wrestling literally, and won't use their body, even when they see you doing it. It's perfectly acceptable to use this technique, and also a perfect way to finish off a stubborn opponent.

Fisticuffs – give

I'm not a fighter. This doesn't mean I've never been in a fight, of course. It means that I'm a decent-sized bloke who gets mellow instead of gobby when I drink, I don't flirt with other blokes' women, and I rarely take the mick. Besides, I think people who like to fight are morons. There is very little satisfaction in hurting another person, even a dyed-in-the-wool arsehole. And if you're a fairly strong person, there's always the possibility of causing permanent damage, death or litigation. Plus, it messes your hand up something rotten when you hit someone in the head.

And then there's the flip side. There are bad people out there, people who will hurt you in any way, shape or form available to them. To assume these people will fight fairly, or refrain from using a pool cue or beer bottle, is a guaranteed way to end up in the hospital or morgue.

Unfortunately, walking away from a fight is difficult for blokes, who often feel passivity constitutes weakness. Yet the best advice is also the simplest: don't fight unless you absolutely have to. Sometimes, though, it comes down to fists, and there's just no getting around it. And while the best advice is avoidance, the second-best advice is to become totally pissed off. Going into a fight half-arsed is a guaranteed way to get your front teeth handed to you. There is no grey area; fight hard or not at all.

Watch just about any action movie, and you'll see the hero use all sorts of uppercuts, roundhouses and big looping punches to knock out his enemies. The only punch you, Joe 'Bloodsports' Bloggs, need is a jab. Sounds weak, but you have to remember you're not wearing boxing

cont.....

gloves. A simple jab, thrown straight from the shoulder, hurts like hell when it lands. And just like a straight thrust in fencing, it's the hardest punch to block. Nearly every amateur fight I've ever been involved in or witnessed has involved more wrestling than boxing, and a jab is also the easiest punch to administer in close quarters fighting. A compact uppercut is also effective, though generally difficult to bring past your opponent's chest. Many fights end up on the ground, and it's tough to bring those big roundhouses into effect when you're rolling around in the pub car park.

It's a rare person who can end a fight with a single punch. A jab can be quickly repeated, and multiple throws are pretty much the name of the game. Two or three well-placed jabs can calm down even the most unruly drunk or loudmouthed, aggressive troublemaker. If you need proof of how effective jabs are, watch an ice hockey game on cable. These nutters know how to bare-knuckle fight, and you'll rarely see a big looping swing. They keep their elbows tucked in and their swings compact, economical. They're also pretty effective at drawing blood in a short time frame.

Make sure you don't tuck your thumb into your palm when you make a fist. If you hit someone like this, the only thing you're going to break is your thumb. Worse, you won't want to hit the person you're fighting again – but he may not be ready to quit. And for God's sake, keep your wrist straight. Bending your wrist up when you punch looks incredibly silly and doesn't work, yet lots of inexperienced fighters do this very thing, usually out of panic.

A lot of people equate that angled wrist with a sissy punch, but the real difference between a punch and a sissy punch is the action of your shoulders and hips. A sissy punch is arm-only. A real punch is simply an extension of your body mass, flung through your hips and shoulders and extended into your arm. By harnessing all the weight of your body, even an eight stone kid can land a serious blow.

Listen, you should only throw a punch as a last resort. But when you feel like you're in danger, when there's no way out of trading blows, hit first and hit hard. It takes a lot to stop certain people, and you never know who you're up against. People get killed and seriously hurt in fights all the time, so this isn't a recommendation to beat someone senseless. The legal and moral arguments against that are obvious and I won't even attempt to address them here. But if someone's going to get hurt, it shouldn't be you. Hit them hard enough to take away their desire to grapple with you, and both of you can wake up in the morning with only minor regrets.

Bottom line: fight only if you have to, but if you have to, don't be a victim. Hit hard, hit fast and then get the hell out of there. Lastly, remember: never punch a girl. And don't punch like a girl either if you can help it.

Fisticuffs – receive

You'd better know what time it is before you get in a fight. No, I don't mean it's 'Hammer Time!', and neither do I mean look at your watch – look at the bloke you're about to fight. If he's not wearing a watch, see which hand he's using to hold his drink. The cleanest punches I've seen have come from lefties (who, incidentally, usually wear their watch on their right wrist and hold their drink in their left hand). Most people don't understand that the southpaw they've just insulted is already in a fighting stance. They're still waiting for the person to rotate when suddenly the punch comes flying out of nowhere and they end up with a bloody lip.

Regardless of your opponent's dominant arm, it's essential that you don't wait for a punch to come to you. Your odds are much better if you're aggressive, or at least moving instead of just standing there. If possible, immediately circle toward your opponent's dominant hand. This shortens and weakens any punch he can throw at you. Protect your groin, gut and eyes – getting hit in any of these places can end a fight and mark the beginning of a beating. If you do get hit in the gut or groin, swivel away instead of bending down, which is a great way to end up with a knee to the face.

Usually the best defence is a good offence. Throwing punches at your opponent's face will keep him disoriented and affect his aim and depth judgment. This is why most street fights end up with about a five per cent hit rate; each bloke is so busy avoiding the other bloke's punches that he rushes his own punches. This is generally a good thing for both parties. After all, there's a simple reason bare-knuckle fighting was banned. These tips might help, but sooner or later you're going to get hit. It hurts. It hurts badly. Get over it.

This isn't just tough bloke talk. It's easy to get paralyzed when someone lands a hard punch, and there will be a desire to retreat, to duck and cover until you can recover. This is the worst way to recover, actually. You need to forget about the pain, to turn it into anger that you can use to your advantage. Shake it off. Give him a bloody smile and wade back in. Sometimes this is more unnerving than landing a telling punch of your own. Don't freak out – people have been smacking each other ever since Gog took more than his share of mammoth meat.

Move with your opponent's punch. This seems obvious and is usually an instinctive avoidance responsive. Nevertheless, many people move into a punch; that is, they lead with their chin, and these are the people who get knocked down with single punches. If you need to move into the other fighter's space, cover your face and tense your stomach muscles.

But unless you're a martial arts guru, moving straight toward your opponent is risky. It's like shooting fairground ducks – all your opponent has to do is lean back and fire away.

If you hit the ground, roll out of the way and get up immediately. Don't expect mercy – expect to get hit or kicked while you're down. If you are getting smacked around, now might be the time to quit boxing and start wrestling. In other words, tackle your opponent, which will reduce

cont.....

the effectiveness of his punches. Go for his waist, not his legs; it's too easy for someone to shake a leg free and put the boot into you.

Taking a fight to the ground also softens the blows you'll receive, which is sort of an added bonus. Of course, the trick here is to avoid being pinned, where your opponent can punch you in various places at his leisure.

Bottom line: if you throw a punch, one or more is going to be thrown back at you. If you're scared or angry enough, most punches you take will be manageable. Not pleasant, but manageable. If you're looking to liven up a dull night by being a bell-end and picking a fight, those punches are going to hurt a lot more. And that's a lesson all in itself.

COPING WITH THE GREAT OUTDOORS

Build a fire in bad weather

A lot of blokes pride themselves on being able to build a fire. They gather up their newspaper and cardboard, their kindling and their dry, split wood, and head down to the bottom of the garden with their butane lighter and some old 'reading material' they've been meaning to get rid of since the 1980s.

This isn't a bad thing. I've done it myself, on more than one occasion. But these are leisure fires. When you really need a fire, when you're wet or cold, a fire isn't just something to melt marshmallows and cremate sausages over. It's a source of life, a means of preventing hypothermia and frostbite. This is almost always the time when a fire is the most difficult to build. There may be snow on the ground, or it might be raining with a strong wind. At times like these, it's essential to know where and how to build a fire quickly.

The first and perhaps most important decision is where to locate your fire. In some cases this will be an easy decision, or circumstances will demand that you build a fire at a certain spot. But if you have a choice, build the fire behind some type of windbreak, such as a large boulder. Locate your fire four to six feet away from the windbreak; the area between the fire and the windbreak will be the warmest spot once everything gets going, and you'll want to be able to occupy it.

Forget the panoramic view and locate the fire close to a decent supply of firewood. If you don't have an axe or handsaw, this means an area of the locality where there's plenty of dead wood. Usually the densest stands of woods have the highest supply of dead wood, since overcrowding tends to kill off some of the trees. If you've read your Jack London, you know to not build a fire under a snow-laden pine tree. The fire can heat up the snow, sending it cascading down to smother your fire. In fact, never build a fire under any pine tree, as they can go up in flames in seconds and you don't want a fire you can't control.

Now that you have a location picked out, try to find some hand-sized rocks for the fire bed (not the traditional fire ring). A properly constructed fire bed facilitates airflow under your fire, much like grating in a wood furnace. This also elevates your fire, reducing contact with damp ground or snow. If you can't locate any rocks, situate some sticks in a row for your fire's base, leaving small gaps between the wood.

cont.....

Now you need to find some kindling. If it's wet, much of the ground material is going to be impossible to light. Two easy sources of elevated kindling are birch bark and the small dead branches found at the base of mature pines. These two materials are commonly found and will light in even the wettest conditions. Birch bark is naturally resistant to water (think birch-bark canoes) and is extremely flammable. The branches at the base of mature pines remain relatively sheltered for years, since the pine tree acts as a huge umbrella. These dead sticks make for excellent kindling. Rotted stumps or logs can also be kicked apart to reveal the dry and often crumbly interiors. These chunks of wood, sometimes scored with insect tunnels, also make excellent kindling in any weather.

Gather enough wood to last at least an hour before you light the kindling, since fledgling fires often fizzle out if left untended during that crucial first stage. The smallest, most flammable kindling goes on the bed of rocks or sticks, with small twigs leaning against each other in a pyramid. The pyramid technique allows the next stage – be it newspaper, cardboard, or bark – to remain loose and uncompressed. Again, this increases airflow, allowing the fire to catch and expand quickly.

Light the fire from the bottom at several locations, to produce a short, intense burst of flame. Waterproof matches or a butane lighter wrapped in a sealed plastic bag have saved many lives over the years, and it's always a good idea to carry one or the other when you're venturing into the woods. Larger kindling goes over the base kindling, again in a pyramid style.

Don't put any heavy stuff on until the smaller material catches, and then only carefully. You don't want to crush the air flow. Be patient, and make sure you have enough smaller kindling to catch that initial wave of fire. A successful fire is built in incremental steps, moving slowly up through kindling sizes until you have arm-sized wood burning steadily.

In extremely cold weather, build an additional two or three fires in a circle if you can, and then sit in the centre. This method will warm you up much quicker than huddling over a single, larger blaze. If you're forced to spend the night and the ground is cold or frozen, build a secondary fire over the area where you plan to sleep. When you get sleepy, put the fire out and sleep on top of the fire-warmed earth. If you don't have the resources to build another fire, use pine boughs or dead grass as a rough mattress to get off the cold, heat-robbing ground.

Pitch a tent

To avoid campsite frustration, put your tent together in your back garden first and carry it with you ready-pitched on your hike. What? Oh no, sorry. Purchase a pack of different-coloured tapes or paints beforehand, then give each joint a unique colour. Later, when the time comes to pitch your tent after a long hike or drive, your tired mind can just follow the colour scheme instead of the directions, which tend to be written in small print by an illiterate bloke who dropped out of engineering college.

Most tents come with a two-tier roof system. The peak will be vented, and the rain flysheet will be suspended slightly over the screened vent. This keeps rain out, while still allowing condensation to exit the tent, so be sure to adjust the rain fly correctly. Otherwise you might have an inadvertent shower (no rain fly) or sauna (rain fly not suspended high enough) in your tent.

Set up your tent on high, level ground. It is an immutable law of nature that rain will fall within four hours of tent pitching, and any small depression will accumulate water. This means a midnight soaking. If you're really unlucky, high winds will accompany that downpour, which can flatten an unsecured tent in seconds. String guy ropes to stakes or trees from each corner. Believe me, you don't want to wake up at three in the morning with a face full of wet nylon. Well, sometimes this isn't such a bad thing, but... never mind.

Make sure you clear the tent base of rocks and branches. This not only prevents the bottom of the tent from ripping, but also makes for a more comfortable night's sleep. If it's cold out and you don't have a cot or air mattress, pile dead grass or soft boughs underneath the tent; you'll stay much warmer if you avoid direct contact with the ground.

Finally, site your campfire upwind and at least ten to fifteen feet away from your tent. This prevents smoke from saturating your tent, and eliminates the possibility of a tent fire; sparks can quickly ignite even 'fireproof' tent material, with disastrous results. The safest bet is to extinguish your fire when you go to bed, but many people like to watch their campfire as they nod off. Just keep the fire a safe distance away from the tent and don't add a load of fuel before you go to sleep.

Happy camping!

Clean a fish

There's an old saying along the lines of 'if you catch it, you clean it'. Thankfully it only applies to fishing and is not the standard advice from the Chief Medical Officer. It often seems easier catching that elusive fish than producing a boneless fillet. Actually, cleaning a fish is easy and sort of fun. It just takes a little practice. And while there are several different ways to clean a fish, from a simple gill-and-gut to the boneless fillet, none of them are very difficult.

Gutting and gilling is a part of steaking, so we'll cover that technique first. Even if you plan on filleting the fish later, gilling and gutting helps preserve flavour and prevent spoilage. Cut from the vent upward until you reach the jaw, being careful to cut only deep enough to sever the muscle tissue and not the guts. Then pull everything out. What, you thought you weren't going to get your hands dirty? Is you a man, or is you a hand model? Rip 'em out of there. The kidneys are two long strips of bloodlike material near the top of the abdominal cavity, along each side of the spine. Use your knife to scrape them off, then reach in and pull the gills out, or just cut the whole head off. Once the guts and head/gills are gone, simply cut the fish crossways to steak it out. If you're going to grill or smoke the fish, this is all you have to do.

Unfortunately, this technique is not the most eater-friendly version of fish cleaning. However, it works well at preserving every ounce of tasty meat on smaller fish like sardines, which are notoriously hard to fillet without wasting meat. To remove scales, use a fish scaler or spoon to scrape off the scales, working from the tail toward the head. Then fry or grill the fish with the skin attached. The skin is edible and actually pretty tasty. However this won't work with trout or any other fish that lacks these larger scales.

That leaves us with the boneless fillet. Nothing but mouthfuls of sweet, crumbly goodness. This is the best way to eat fish, and also the most involved cleaning technique. Not hard, mind you, just more involved than other methods. Lay the fish flat on its side. The knife goes in just behind the pectoral fin and the operculum, angled straight down or slightly toward the head. Cut into the fish until you reach the spine, then turn the blade so it's parallel with the backbone. Keeping the blade flat, run the knife along the spine, being careful to avoid cutting through the backbone. You should feel the knife cutting through the ribs, which will dull most fillet knives pretty quickly. Be sure to re-sharpen your knife after every two or three fish.

Stop about an inch before the base of the tail, right before the meat runs out. Then flip the fillet over, so the skin is facing down. Now slide the knife edge between the skin and the meat, just above the tail, and gently saw your way up through the fillet. Keep pressure on the skin with the flat of the knife blade. You may want to press your free hand down on the skin to keep it from tearing. A gentle back and forth sawing motion works best to remove the skin from the fillet. You should end up with a hunk of skin still attached to the fish, and one skinless fillet.

Now slide the knife behind the rib cage of the fillet and cut out the ribs, keeping the knife edge pressed against the back of the ribcage to prevent waste. Some fish will have centre bones behind the ribcage that run back to the tail, and other fish may have additional bones embedded in the fillet. Run your thumb back and forth over the fillet to find any bones that you missed. You might also want to remove the strip of dark red meat along the lateral line (straight down the middle of the outside of the fillet). This meat often has a strong, unpleasant taste. It's fairly soft, so just scrape it off with the knife edge.

Run rapids

Rapids – those frothy, treacherous, often boulder-filled stretches of fast water – are a major part of what canoeing is all about. They can also wreck a canoe in seconds. The key to staying dry and having fun is planning out your route through the rapids beforehand. For bigger rapids, or long runs, beach the canoe upstream, then walk downstream to get an idea of where your best route lies.

That said, very few pre-planned routes go exactly as planned. 'Stay the course' is not an option, and missing one arc of your route can mean all subsequent plans are suddenly useless. When you do stray from the planned course, it's essential that you communicate clearly with your partner. Usually, the person in the bow will call the shots, while the person in the back supplies most of the steering power. It's essential that both of you know what it means when the bow yells 'Right!' Does it mean there's a rock on the right, or does it mean go right? Confusion results in midstream pirouettes, tip-overs, and smashed canoes.

You can usually spot submerged rocks by their boils. If the boil is frothy, the rock is usually just underneath the surface. Deeper rocks will usually have smoother boils, though sometimes a flat-topped rock just underneath the surface will have a smooth boil. The deepest water is also usually where the fastest current flows, so following the main runs generally equals the smoothest ride.

If you do get hung up on a rock, it's almost impossible to push the canoe back upstream to free yourself. Instead, push off to one side, being careful to avoid a sideways flip. If you push far enough out into the current, the water will often grab the canoe and swing you off the rock. Unfortunately, this also means you might end up traversing the rapids backward. On the upside, you get to see a lot of amused faces from the paddlers behind you as you try to turn back around.

Chop down a tree

Notching and felling a tree is a simple matter of primary school physics, but every year people are killed when the tree they're cutting falls on top of them. Countless more wannabe lumberjacks drop trees on their cars, houses, neighbour's dog, and so forth. Standard fare for yawnsome *You've Been Framed* vids, but a nightmare on insurance premiums.

Assess the tree before you start cutting. Is it leaning in a direction you don't want it to go? Is it surrounded by other trees that might hang it up once it falls? Is it dead on top? If so, could the brittle upper section snap off once it starts to fall? The term for a tree like this is a widow maker, and they've killed a lot of would-be lumberjacks.

If possible, work with the unique conditions of each tree. If it's leaning hard to the south, drop it that way. If it grows straight up, but there's a strong wind (and don't underestimate wind power – the canopy of a tree can act like a sail, even if it's fairly calm at ground level), fell the tree in the same direction the wind is blowing. If you can't drop it the way conditions dictate – if, for example, there's a house in the way – attach two ropes as high up on the tree as possible, and have a couple of helpers pull on each rope at quartering angles. The tree should fall between them, but make sure your helpers are at least as far away as the tree is tall.

Okay, now that we know where we want the tree to go, let's knock this bugger down. First, make sure the area around the base of the tree is clear of underbrush, logs, or any other debris that might get in your way. No matter how well you plan, sometimes you just need to drop the chainsaw and run like hell. Cut the brush away and clear out any debris before you start working on the tree.

Never cut down a tree by sawing straight through, since the tree will lean forward and pinch the chainsaw bar between the stump and the still-standing tree. With a larger tree, it's almost impossible to free the bar of a stuck chainsaw without cutting the tree down with an axe or another chainsaw. Instead, notch out a wedge on the same side you want the tree to fall, no more than halfway through the tree. Remove the wedge, then simply cut down at an angle from the opposite side.

The tree will usually fall in the direction of the wedge, although it's possible for it to fall in any direction. Stop often to push gently on the tree with your shoulder to guide it in the right direction when you're making the final cut. When it starts to fall, shut off the chainsaw and move away. Kickbacks, falling limbs, and an idling chainsaw are a recipe for disaster when trees start to fall.

Make sure the tree is all the way down before moving in for limbing and sectioning. Sometimes other trees, undergrowth, or the branches will keep the tree suspended for a moment before it actually comes to its final rest. These secondary falls are rarely fatal, but can crush a foot in an instant, so look out. Not worth £250 off whoever replaced Beadle, that's for sure.

Track something

There's one cardinal rule with tracking. You have to slow down. Since there is often adrenaline flowing during a tracking situation, it's easy to rush things. But you can't rush a trail unless you have absolutely perfect conditions, and then only at your own peril. It's easy to assume you can't lose the track, only to have it disappear, or end up tracking the wrong animal (or person for that matter).

The trail as you first approach it is unbroken, as clear as it will ever be. Don't ruin that by stamping back and forth. Always mark the location you first saw the animal by noting two or three landmarks, a process commonly referred to as triangulation. This is an extremely useful tool to locate an area first viewed from a distance. Once you locate the first track, look for the second, third, and so on. This will establish a line of travel, which can be deceiving from a distance. Then mark the location of the first track. Just shove a stick into the ground, or hang a glove from a tree. That way you'll always have a starting point if you end up losing the track. Keep doing this each time the terrain changes into less trackable conditions – such as a stretch of dry ground or the confluence of other tracks with your own.

Walk parallel to the tracks, close enough to see them clearly but not on top of them. If you lose sight of the tracks, mark the last track and then move out in increasing circles until you pick it up again. Don't rush. In fact, if you're applying this tracking technique to a hunting situation, you shouldn't even begin tracking until 30 minutes after your shot, since an animal that's pushed after a shot will go much farther than an animal allowed to rest and stiffen up.

Most wounded animals will head downhill and/or into thick cover. If there's a sizable dell or stream nearby, most animals will instinctively head toward it, even if they're a mile or more away. In some cases, it's a good idea to circle ahead of the animal if it looks like it's going to cross a stream that you can't. Otherwise, move slowly and don't leave the trail.

If you end up tracking in the dark, a lantern is much more effective than a torch. The soft, even light works well to pick up blood spoor, and it casts a wider sphere of light than a narrow-beamed torch. If you're tracking without snow and without blood spoor, things get tough in a hurry. Following broken blades of grass or overturned pebbles is the stuff of fiction for most amateur trackers. Instead, try to determine a line of movement for the animal, then concentrate on those areas where it's possible to pick up a track (e.g., a muddy flat or a meadow of tall grass that will bend as the animal passes). Look for overturned leaves, which are often easy to spot in older-growth forests, since they expose bare earth when the animal passes by.

This sporadic tracking technique can be tricky, but it often works if you have a basic understanding of what's driving the animal. Is it fear? Hunger? Anxiety? Maybe the need to mate? Stop and think about the reasons the animal is moving and where it might find what it's after. Then use the trackable areas to confirm or reject your hypothesis.

Remember also that tracking conditions can dictate how long you have to track. Falling snow means great tracking, but if you fall too far behind, the tracks will fill in. The same principle applies to heavy frost or dew, which will disappear as the day wears on. Adjust your tracking rate accordingly.

Transplant trees and shrubs

Gardens worldwide are covered with dead and dying transplanted trees. There are usually only two living things involved in the transplant: the tree and the bloke who planted it. Guess who's to blame? The number one cause of transplant death is dehydration. Every time a root is exposed to air, cells begin to die. This severely affects the tree's ability to absorb water, and a cut or broken root exacerbates the problem. And while small roots may seem unimportant, they often have more surface area than the larger roots, which lack the numerous root tendrils essential for water and nutrient uptake. A successful transplant, then, means minimizing damage to the entire root system. This is accomplished by keeping the roots damp and protected.

While most purchased trees and shrubs have their root system in pretty good shape, hand-dug transplants are often DOA, even if they look fine for a few days. The reason these trees don't survive is because their root system has been severed too close to the trunk, with the smaller but essential roots cut away. The circle of sod from a dug transplant should be at least equal to the diameter of the tree's canopy. If you're digging up a sapling with vertically oriented branches, carefully bend one of the main limbs to the side to get an idea of where the root system ends. Digging up this much sod limits your ability to transplant big trees, of course.

Mark the north side of the tree with a piece of tape or a plastic tie before you lift it out of the ground. When you drop it into the new hole, make sure that part of the tree faces north again. Trees often have different morphology on their sunny and shade sides, and switching exposure causes unnecessary stress.

The new hole should be a few inches wider than the tree's base of roots, since cramming a tree in a small hole will cause the root ends to point up or break, reducing water uptake. If the soil is hard, use a shovel or rake to loosen the soil at the bottom of the hole, then dump a bucket of water over the freshly turned soil. This will provide a soft, damp bed for the roots to thread into those crucial first weeks. A layer of wetted potting soil can be substituted, and also provides extra nutrients.

Make sure you fill any gaps with soil and loose strips of sod to retain moisture. It is nearly impossible to overwater a shrub or tree during those first few weeks; it is woefully easy to underwater them. Many people don't realize how much water it takes to soak through to the root system, nor do they realize how quickly loose soil can dry out. Remember, the transplanted roots are functioning very inefficiently at first, and they need to be surrounded by wet soil constantly for the tree to live.

The need for water will remain constant for about a year. While daily waterings aren't necessary after the first few weeks, transplanted trees can't handle long periods of dry weather until the root system is fully developed. Water accordingly.

Graft a tree

I distinctly remember being amazed when I first learned that every single Granny Smith apple originally came from a single tree. The same goes for Braeburns, Golden Delicious and basically every other tree fruit you can find in the shops. You can't pop the seeds out of that crispy apple and stick them in a pot, since apple trees cross-pollinate with other apple trees, even if they're crab apples. The resulting offspring will usually produce apples quite unlike their parent stock and are usually inedible. In fact, the odds of finding an edible – not tasty, just edible – apple from a seed is somewhere around a thousand to one.

Instead of relying on those odds, the earliest fruit growers started grafting trees to produce clones of the mother tree. To do this, you cut a branch, commonly called a scion, from the parent tree and join it to a root from another strain of tree from the same species. In fact, almost every fruit tree you see is actually two trees; from the ground up it's the tasty fruit-bearing strain, and underground it's a hardy, disease resistant rootstock. If you look closely, you can usually see a slight bend or twist in the trunk of any fruit tree, just above the ground. This is where the two sections were joined. Grafting a tree allows you to maintain a desirable line, or even develop your own strain of fruit. It's also much cheaper than buying trees from the nursery.

Start about six to eight weeks before the growing season by ordering a good, hardy rootstock via any tree nursery catalogue. You can also buy the branch, or scion, or snip some from the trees you already have. It should be a young scion, with four buds or less, and harvested during winter. The rootstock and the scion should be about the same diameter. You'll also need a sharp knife, masking or electrical tape, and paraffin wax.

The method I most commonly use is the whip graft. To do this, you cut the rootstock and the scion at about a 30-degree angle. Use a very sharp knife (dull ones crush the delicate cambium layer) and make an angled cut in one smooth motion through the rootstock. Then cut straight down through the middle of the angle, about as deep as the knife blade. Repeat this on the scion, again cutting fast and clean through the tissue at the same angle, then notching it longitudinally in the centre. Quickly snug the two pieces together to prevent cell damage. It's vitally important that the rootstock and scion match in diameter and angle to get the best seal.

Now wrap the two sections together with electrical or masking tape or an asphalt/water emulsion glue, commonly sold at garden centres and nurseries. If you use tape, wrap it securely, but don't apply too much pressure. Just like over-tightening a tourniquet, applying too much pressure will cut off the life-giving liquid (sap instead of blood). Apply some paraffin wax over the tape to prevent dehydration and disease.

Wrap with damp paper towels, then damp newspaper, and finally a layer of dry newspaper. Then refrigerate. Leave the grafts alone for six to eight weeks in the fridge, watering occasionally to keep the roots damp. Once you see the root formation poke out, go ahead and plant the tree. Be extremely diligent with your watering schedule. Your success rate is not going to be 100 per cent, so you'll want to do this in batches of at least ten.

Dress and quarter large game

Anyone who pulls the trigger on an animal had better know how to clean it, and clean it quickly. You owe the animal that at least. Prompt field dressing is essential in preserving taste and preventing spoilage, especially in warmer weather, but some hunters worry too much about the shot, and not enough about the plate.

You're going to get your hands bloody. Once you accept that, everything is pretty straightforward. Despite all the weekend warriors who walk around with Bowie knives strapped to their waists, there's actually not much heavy cutting involved. All you need is a three- to four-inch knife with a good, thick blade. A meat saw is nice, too.

Lay the animal so the belly is facing up or to the side. You may want to cut a branch long enough to prop the animal's rear legs open, which will make for easier cutting. Cut from the vent to the bottom of the rib cage, exactly in the middle of the belly – but don't cut deep! Cutting too deep will puncture internal organs, including the intestines, stomach, and bladder.

The contents of these organs are not something you want on your steaks. Cut all the way around the vent, and lop off any dangling reproductive structures. Cut through the meat above the pelvic arch to reveal the pelvic bone, which needs to be split or cut open. Since deer have hard bones, you may need to use a small saw to cut through the pelvis. Sometimes it's possible to use the point of your knife as a wedge to split the pelvic bone, though this is tricky in older or heavy-boned animals.

Now that everything is opened up, all you have to do is pull the viscera – okay, let's just call them guts – out. Cut all the way around the vent in order to free the end of the large intestine. Everything below the diaphragm should pull free easily, though you may need to do a little cutting to free the kidneys and connective tissue. There should be more pulling than cutting. Use your knife to cut out the diaphragm, which is a large thin flap of muscle separating the guts from the heart and lungs, then cut the heart and lungs free (they're attached near the front of the chest cavity) and pull the whole works loose.

If you have a large animal on the ground, and no vehicle nearby, you're going to need to quarter the animal before hauling it out. It's best to try and hang the animal from a tree before quartering (it's much easier to field dress them this way, too).

Remove the head just below the base of the skull, and then the legs at the knee joints. Starting from the tail, use a meat saw to cut through the exact middle of the spine, which will result in two equal halves. It's important to stay in the middle of the spine, even though it means lots of cutting. To quarter the animal, cut through the second or third rib from the bottom. If you have a really heavy animal, you can cut it into sixths or even eighths. If you're going to drag the quarters out, leave the hide on. Otherwise, skin the animal to reduce weight.

Once the animal is field dressed, move the meat to a cool location as soon as possible. Wild game is remarkably flavourful if handled and cooked correctly, but mistreatment at the initial stages of butchering can often result in a 'gamey' taste. Just remember to dive in and get it cleaned – blood washes off.

Operate reels

Of the two common fishing reels, spincast reels are generally easier to operate, especially for lighter tackle. The reel hangs down from the rod, and you reel with your left hand (for right-handed people). To cast this type of reel, hold the line against the base of the rod with your right index finger then flip open the bail with your left hand.

Bring the rod back with your right hand, then bring it forward and release the line with your finger. Once the lure hits the water, simply flip the bail back over and start reeling. If reeling with your left hand feels too awkward, you can easily switch the handle around so you reel with your dominant hand. Just unscrew the handle, slide it out, and reinsert from the other end. While this makes it easier to reel, it also weakens your hook-setting power, since you're now relying on your non-dominant hand for the hook-set.

If you're fishing for twitchy fish with live bait, you can leave the bail open so it can take your offering without feeling resistance. Make sure the line catches in the groove at the base of the bail when you flip it back over. If it doesn't catch, the line will flip the bail back up when you try to set the hook, and you'll end up losing a lot of fish.

The downside to using a spincast reel is the drag. The drag is the adjustable tension in your reel, used to automatically give line once a certain pressure is attained. Ideally, the drag is set just below the breaking point of your line, which means you can exert the maximum pressure on the fish without breaking the line. With spincast reels, the drag is usually either at the base or top of the reel, making mid-catch adjustments tricky.

Baitcast reels, on the other hand, have an inherently smooth drag, and this is located on the side of the reel for easy adjustment. These attributes make baitcast reels ideal for bigger fish, and are almost always used over spincast reels for big-water sportfishing. Baitcast reels, however, are generally more difficult to cast. The spindle holding the line spins as line goes out, and it doesn't stop when the lure does. It keeps on spinning, and unless you stop it with your thumb, a backlash will result. A backlash resembles a giant bird's nest of tangled line, and generally only happens when the fish are in a feeding frenzy. They take approximately five hours to untangle.

To avoid backlashes, keep the pad of your thumb on the spool as the lure nears the water. Apply pressure just as, or right before, the lure hits the water. This stops the spool from spinning, which in turn prevents that dreaded backlash. Most baitcast reels come with an adjustable spool control, which adjusts the spool spin rate. Imagine this option as a type of brake, which can make the spool very resistant to spin or, when set on low, will cause only a slight drag. You'll get better casting distance with less resistance, but will be more prone to backlashes. Just experiment a bit to find the right combination for the reel you're using.

Cast a fly rod

Throwing a fly at a rising fish is pure and simple fun. Besides the obvious thrill of seeing a fish slurp a fly off the surface, fish put up a terrific fight on a fly rod. Just ask J.R. Hartley. Poor old sod can hardly move any more – he just sits in his armchair making nuisance calls to people chosen at random from the Yellow Pages.

A typical dry fly, complete with steel hook, weighs roughly nothing. Most fly-fishing occurs in shallow water, where fish are easily frightened, so you'll need to throw this speck of feathers and thread a considerable distance, sometimes upward of 50 feet. Since the fly weighs next to nothing, you accomplish this by using the weight and momentum of the line, not the lure.

The fly is attached to a leader, typically tapered monofilament six to ten feet long. The leader attaches directly to the fly line, which is weighted. You can use floating or sinking-tip fly line, depending on if you're fishing on the surface or below it, a common way to fish nymphs or streamers. The fly line is attached to backing, or tough braided line that usually remains on the reel.

For the best results, have 30 feet or more of level clearance in front of and behind you. Wading out into a shallow lake or river is perfect. It's easiest to cast at a diagonal angle to increase the backcasting area behind you. If you want to practice at home, just stand in your front garden or the local park and remove the fly from the end of the leader.

Strip out about six feet of line and hold the excess with your left hand. You can strip out more line and let it pool in front of you, but you'll be more prone to tangles. Hold the rod in your right hand, and use your index finger to hold the line just above the reel. Grip the excess line in your left hand, then lift the tip of the fly rod up so the weighted line is just off the water. Now you're ready for your first cast.

Move your arm back to the two o'clock position, lifting the flyline off the water, while still holding the excess line in your other hand. As the line unfurls behind you, you'll feel the weight of the line going back. Right before it stops, simply move your arm forward to the ten o'clock position, which will propel the line forward. Try to keep your elbow level, like it's sliding along a shelf. Once the line straightens out in front of you, let out some of the excess line and lower your rod tip. The line should set down gently on the water.

Since most fly rods are seven to nine feet long, with a similar length of leader material, this means your fly is now roughly 20 to 25 feet in front of you. This is plenty for most fishing, and there's no need for false casting (repeated passes of the fly line to build up distance).

If you do need to go further, don't set the rod tip down. Instead, wait until the line unfurls in front of you and then draw it back again, stripping more line off the reel with your left hand and feeding the slack into the back loop. Repeat this process until you're out far enough or you get

cont.....

tangled up, whichever comes first. Be warned, though – repeat this more than three or four times, and the line gets difficult to handle. Don't false cast just because you think it looks cool.

If you're casting in running water, cast slightly upstream of the area where the fish are rising. Be sure to lift the rod tip as the fly drifts downstream, which prevents the line from bellying and creating an unnatural drag on the fly. Be sure to keep the slack at a minimum, since a quick hook-set is essential. Many fish will spit a fly back out once they realize it tastes like feathers and glue. (Wait 'til they try the output of my local Southern Fried Chicken then...)

There's no need to stick with dry flies, either. Nymphs, an imitation of a larval insect, are deadly on stream fish. Streamers, which mimic swimming invertebrates or small minnows, can be cast out and slowly reeled back in by hand-stripping. Whatever you use, be sure to run it by you on the water a few times to get an idea of how it looks and moves in the water.

Remove a fish hook from your body

Removing a hook you've hilariously embedded in your hide yourself is cheaper and faster than going to a doctor, and it's a lot less embarrassing, too. It also hurts like hell, but if you're deep in the middle of nowhere and far from a doctor, it's usually less painful to remove it yourself than wait for someone else to do it for you. So pull yourself together lad, and get a good grip.

Pulling a barbed hook out the way it went in is incredibly difficult, hurts very badly, and can cause a lot of bleeding. A much better way is to push the hook out, snip off the barb, and retract it. This is easier with bigger hooks, since they have a larger bend and are consequently easier to turn back out through the skin. If the hook is attached to a lure with more than one set of hooks, be sure to remove the extra set of hooks first. It's all too easy to double – or treble – your trouble when the twitching and the swearing starts in earnest.

Let it bleed for at least a minute after you pull the hook out. Puncture wounds are notoriously prone to infection, and blood naturally rinses the hole, removing rust and bacteria present on the hook. Then bandage it up and go stagger back into the tent to sleep it off.

What – you didn't just pull that out while you were sober, did you?

Equip and maintain a boat

There is nothing, absolutely nothing half so much worth doing as simply messing about in boats. So said a talking rat. I for one completely agree. So how do you go about the basics of running a boat?

First, you've got to deal with the engine. Many outboard boat motors still operate on two-cycle technology. This means a certain amount of oil is mixed right into the petrol. Depending on the make and model, you may have to mix the petrol yourself (usually 50 parts petrol to one part two-cycle oil), or you may have to fill up an oil reservoir (oil-injected models). Make sure you know the right way to fuel up – adding the wrong fuel mixture is an easy way to ruin an expensive boat motor.

Like a lot of small engines, it's not a good idea to use ethanol blends in your boat motor. This type of fuel can gum up your carburettor pretty quickly. And when you're on the water, a stalled outboard motor is a bit more serious than having a breakdown on the motorway with your car.

Many boats don't come equipped with what veteran sailors would consider essential boat equipment. Just as you wouldn't embark on a long road trip without a good spare tyre, neither should you head out on the water without some standard boat equipment and some quick-fix knowledge.

- **BOAT PLUG** Yeah, this is a pretty essential piece of equipment. Make sure it's in place before you drop the boat into the water. Forgetting this happens to thousands of boaters every year, even experienced ones. Not me, of course. Never happened, I tell you.

• **BILGE PUMP** This is a submersible pump located in the hull of the boat that pumps water back from whence it came. Use it if you're taking on water from a leak, big waves or a heavy rainstorm. Just leave it on until you're in the clear; most bilge pumps have a float switch that shuts them off when water levels decrease. If you have a bilge pump, check to make sure it's operational by lifting the float switch before you hit big water.

• **WATER INTAKE** If you run your boat through heavy weeds or drag the propeller through a sandbar, the intake can plug up. This will cause the motor to overheat in short order. Turn the engine off and tilt the motor all the way; you'll see a screen just above the propeller, on the side of the shaft. Clean the screen out and lower the motor back into the water. Water should spit out of the port just under the motor, above the waterline. If not, you may need to replace the impeller, a small in-line pump that circulates cooling water through the boat engine. This isn't an on-the-water repair job. Limp it home and replace the impeller before you go back out.

• **ANCHOR** Every boat should have an anchor and at least 100 feet of rope, even if you're not planning on stopping. If your motor stalls and it's a windy day, a good anchor can keep you off the rocks until help arrives or you fix the problem.

Operate a motor boat

STARTING AND RUNNING AN OUTBOARD MOTOR

Starting the engine seems pretty simple, and many times it's simply a matter of turning the key. But if nothing happens, you might not have a dead battery. All outboard and inboard engines won't start if the gear shifter isn't in neutral – a standard safety precaution. Check to make sure you're in neutral, then try it again.

If the battery is dead, you can try to get a jump start from another boat. However, many fishing boats also have a separate trolling motor battery, also called a deep-cycle battery, which can be used to start the motor. Switch the starting battery back once the boat starts. Just don't touch the cables together when you're switching them, and don't shut the motor off for at least 15 minutes, which should be enough time for the alternator to charge up the dead battery.

Many smaller outboards can be started manually with a pull rope (in fact, this is the only option for starting some motors). If there isn't one on the motor, just pop the motor cover off – you'll see the flywheel right on top. Wind the rope (if there isn't an emergency pull rope in the boat, a shoelace sometimes works) around the groove in the flywheel, then yank on it.

If the battery is cranking over fine, but the motor still won't start, squeeze the fuel bulb a few times to make sure you're getting petrol into the carburettor. The fuel bulb is located along the fuel line, usually fairly close to the motor. Squeeze it until it gets hard (get your mind out of the gutter), then try it again.

If it's cold out, or if the motor has been sitting for a while, you'll need to choke the motor. Start out with full choke, but be prepared to quickly shut it down to half-choke; outboards tend to rev extremely high on full choke. If the boat has a hand throttle lever, there's often a button on the pivot point of the throttle lever. Press this button to bring the throttle level forward without engaging the transmission; this means you can rev up the motor without putting it in gear. Just bring the throttle lever back to neutral after the motor is warm. You'll hear a click, which means you can engage the transmission.

HEADING OUT TO SEA

Once you've got the motor started, make sure you cast off any lines holding you to the dock and/or pull up the anchor. Don't accelerate rapidly at landing areas; docking and trailering boats can be a delicate task, and excessive wakes are a pain for other boaters trying to get in or out of the water.

'Getting on plane' is a term that refers to running your boat on the same horizontal plane as the water surface. You'll have to attain a certain speed to 'plane out', but the exact speed depends on boat shape, size and load. You'll want to get up on plane if you're going long distances; running in the diagonal 'bow up' half speed is inefficient and dangerous in big waves, even if you're going slower than you would on plane.

Make sure the motor is in the full-down position. There's usually a thumb lever on the side of the throttle lever on console-driven boats,

which is called the tilt-and-trim button. Tilt and trim are actually the same thing – tilt usually refers to changing motor angles at rest, and trim refers to changing motor angles while on plane.

Many tiller-operated boats [no steering wheel] have a lever at the base of the motor for adjusting the height of the propeller. You can lock the motor in the down position or halfway up – you won't have the full range of positions that automatic [battery-operated] tilt-and-trim motors have. However, one nice option on tiller-operated boats is a release tilt, which lets the motor swing freely if you hit a submerged rock or log.

Once you've got the motor all the way down, accelerate smoothly. The front of the boat will begin to rise, which is normal. Just keep accelerating until the front of the boat comes back down. Now you're on plane, and probably moving fairly quickly across the top of the water. If you have power trim, slowly begin to raise the motor back up. This, in turn, raises the bow [front] of the boat back up. You'll get an increase in speed and fuel efficiency on a properly trimmed boat, because you won't be ploughing through as much water. Learning when to stop raising the motor is dependent on boat style and load, but you can usually hear the motor smooth out when you hit the sweet spot. Just don't raise the motor so much that the prop comes out of the water.

If you encounter big waves, it is imperative to keep the bow pointed into them, either straight on or at a quartering angle. This might mean making a long detour at two oblique angles, but one of the main causes of capsizing is maintaining a course where waves can slam into the side of the boat. Bows are made to handle waves, not sterns or gunwales [backs or sides, respectively] – that's why they're pointed.

HEADING IN FROM SEA

Boats do not have brakes. Putting the motor in neutral only slows you down – and killing the motor is the worst thing you can do; if the motor is running you can at least use the reverse gear to stop or slow your forward progress.

At higher speeds, turning works much better than slowing or stopping when you need to avoid an obstacle. Manoeuvring the boat at slower speeds can actually be more difficult than at higher speeds. Unlike a car, you don't have any friction between your vehicle and the driving surface to make tight turns. The best philosophy is a simple one: move in a predetermined, straight line. This is actually faster than zooming in, reversing, and making frantic adjustments.

Canoe basics

The only way to stay inside a canoe for any length of time is to remain in the centre, keep your body as low as possible, and avoid sudden side-to-side movements. This means you have to stay seated, and you can't lean over the side of the canoe to net a fish, spit or look at your reflection. I've been in tip-overs with people who have done all of 'em, and I've been guilty once or twice myself.

When you step into or out of a canoe, be sure to step exactly in the middle, and get the other person to steady the canoe until you're seated. If it's too shallow to load from the side, load the back of the canoe into the water first, leaving the bow resting lightly on the bank. Have one person steady the canoe while the stern paddler gets seated. Once the stern paddler is seated, he should wedge his paddles into the lake bottom to steady the canoe while the bow paddler gets in. Then gently rock the canoe back into the water.

When exiting, have the person in the bow get out first, while the person in the stern again uses both paddles to steady the canoe. Again, run the bow up on land if possible, which will stabilize the canoe.

Canoes can handle surprisingly big waves, but only with experienced paddlers inside and only when the canoe is running with the waves. Sometimes this means a long detour at right angles to the point you're trying to reach and a lot of hard paddling, but it's still faster than swimming. Trying to take even small waves at cross angles can mean a quick dunking.

Keep all your gear in waterproof containers, since very few canoes arrive at their destination without some water being dripped into the bottom. Even the simple act of switching sides with the paddle can accumulate a lot of water in the bottom of the canoe. A couple of strips of lightweight wood underneath your gear works great to keep everything off the wet bottom, and oversized rubbish bags make great temporary rain jackets for your kit.

Solo paddling is tough, since even a light wind will push the bow around, making it difficult to steer. If you have to paddle alone, place some weight in the front of the canoe. Don't worry about the extra weight; a heavier, well balanced canoe is far easier to navigate than a light, back-heavy one.

Tell direction with a compass

Well, this is easy enough, right? Hold the compass out flat on your palm, far away from any magnetic fields that might cause interference, like batteries or power lines. Then tap it once or twice and wait until the needle swings north. Rotate the compass so that the needle lines up with the north direction, and you know all four directions.

Yeah, but where the hell are you? And in which of the four clearly defined directions do you go? Too many people venture into the woods with a compass and figure they can't get lost. The problem is, they don't have any idea of where they are (they're lost, duh) because they never took a reading before they headed into the woods. They might know where north and south are, but that doesn't help one single bit. About the best a compass can do now is keep them from walking in circles.

A compass is an invaluable tool for navigating through unfamiliar territory, but it needs to be used before you get lost. Use your compass like joggers use a watch, checking in periodically to track your progress. Ascertaining your line of travel isn't just a matter of looking at the needle, though. You need to pick out landmarks in front of and behind your current location. This will allow you to visually draw a line of travel, which you can use to determine the direction that will lead you out of the woods. It is essential to do this frequently so you have a continuous line of landmarks to follow and reference. Coupled with frequent compass checks, it's almost impossible to get lost this way.

If the land is flat and/or heavily wooded, you'll need to stop more often than in hilly or open areas, since landmarks won't be visible for extended periods. Regardless of the terrain, pay attention to the surrounding countryside by designating certain trees, hills or features as landmarks. Take a moment to memorize each one. This keeps you moving in a straight line, and familiarizes you with each area you pass through. If you still get turned around, the odds of finding a familiar sight increase exponentially.

A map, even a cheap roadmap, can work wonders in conjunction with a compass. Again, determine your line of travel before you start, find a couple of landmarks in the distance (even if it's not in the direction you want to go), and mark them on the map. Keep doing this, and odds are you can easily look around at any time and know your general location.

Tell direction without a compass

There are many different ways to tell directions without a compass, all with varying degrees of accuracy. The most consistent markers are the celestial objects, such as the sun and stars. The rising or setting sun is pretty much a no-brainer, but it can be difficult to tell which direction it's heading in the middle of the day or behind heavy clouds. And if you're lost, waiting a couple of hours for the sunset can be excruciating.

If there's enough light to cast a shadow, find an open area and drive a big stick into the ground. Then use another stick to mark the line of the shadow. Wait about 15 minutes, then mark the new line with another stick, approximately half of the way up the shadow. Draw a line between these two sticks for an approximate east-west line.

At night, the easiest way to find north is to look for Polaris, or the North Star. This isn't nearly as tough as it might seem, because all you have to do is locate the Big Dipper. Extend an imaginary line from the end of the Dipper, about four times the depth of the Dipper, to find Polaris. Since it might be hard to remember where north was when daylight comes, line Polaris up with a prominent landmark (e.g. a tall tree or hill), then mark the spot where you're standing. If you can't find a recognizable landmark in the starlight, mark one area on the ground with a stick or rock, then back up about 20 feet, all the while keeping Polaris directly in front of you. Draw a line between your two marks in the morning, and you'll know your north-south line.

A waxing or waning moon is also a great way to tell direction. If the moon rises before sunset, the illuminated side is west. If the moonrise occurs after midnight, the illuminated side is to the east. Got that?

Once you look down on the ground, things get iffy in a hurry. Moss will grow around the entire base of the tree, but will usually be thickest on the north side. Tree branches will be fewer and sparser on the north side, and animals tend to build nests and dens in areas with maximum sunlight exposure, such as south-facing slopes. These clues should be good enough to give you a rough estimate of the direction you need to travel, but are by no means infallible even for a wannabe Crocodile Dundee. Never rely on one clue; instead, use a weight-of-evidence approach.

If you end up lost – and let's face it, if you're inspecting moss depth on tree trunks you're bloody lost – you have to make yourself sit down and relax. In fact, it's usually best to remain right there, since wandering off is the most dangerous thing you can do. Odds are you'll be found in short order.

But if you're deep in the middle of nowhere and nobody's looking for you, it's essential that you keep walking in a straight line, using whatever directions you can gather from your surroundings. Eventually you'll hit a road or a stream, either of which will eventually lead you to civilization.

Understand and work with dogs

Aggressive and uncooperative dogs are just a pain in the neck for everyone – owners, other dogs, posties, you name it. Yet almost every dog can be a useful, devoted pet. The key to turning Well'ard into Lassie involves a simple attitude adjustment – and not just for the dog.

Dogs are pack animals. While many people understand this, they can't seem to grasp another concept: unless you establish dominance over a dog, you are not a respected member of its pack. You are competition, and unless you want to spend the next ten to fifteen years of your life lying belly-up every time Fido comes over, you're going to have a bad relationship with your dog. The key task in forming a successful relationship with any dog is to put it at ease, which essentially means making it feel like it's in a pack situation. If you're the owner, this means establishing a hierarchy, with you at the top.

No matter how much you love your dog, you must be the pack leader, the alpha male or alpha female. This doesn't mean you should beat your dog and then go piss on the corner of his kennel. It simply means that you have to make the dog respect you by dispensing justice in a fair, consistent manner. No need to beat him, but no slacking off, either. Dogs need discipline to function within a family unit. This means not letting them run in the house before you, making sure they listen to you all the time, and setting consequences for bad behaviour. Consistently. It's work, just like parenting, but if you do it correctly, and at an early age, you'll never be one of those sorry plonkers on the canine version of *Super Nanny*.

Unlike children, dogs lack a highly developed sense of emotional remorse. And, while they understand tone and simple words, lengthy discussions about their bad behaviour don't accomplish much. As such, I usually leave the 'I'm so disappointed in you' speech at home. Instead, a couple of moderate smacks across the shoulder or rump usually get, and hold, their attention. Just to be clear: I've always had Labrador retrievers, big, strong animals who are immune to minor physical discomfort and have the learning curve of a stump. For a highly-strung setter or spaniel, or a smaller dog, a swat across the shoulders might not be a good idea. It all depends on the individual dog's temperament, size and age. Avoid using physical punishment on puppies, too, since you don't want to make your dog overly submissive. These pups can turn out like the doggy equivalent of the needy kid at school who always asked where the party was going to be, starting on Tuesday morning.

Treats can be administered for positive behaviour, either food snacks or petting, but don't overdo it. Again, consistency is the key, especially when the dog is young. It sets limits for the dog, and, if done during puppyhood, the dog will rarely, if ever, cross those interior boundaries. Dogs can live ten to fifteen years and are a serious financial and emotional investment. Make sure you spend lots of extra time with them that first couple of years, setting limits, getting the dog to accept its beta role within the household, and basically nipping bad behaviour in the bud. It takes work, but the end result is what every dog owner wants: a good dog who fetches his slippers, eats cats and doesn't mind being dressed up in sunglasses and old school ties occasionally just because it's funny.

Ride a horse

To most weekend riders, the underlying concern when riding a horse is not getting thrown, and not looking like a total Noddy at the reins. The easiest and simplest way to avoid the painful indignity is to pick out a horse with a good disposition. If you have a choice of mounts, pick a horse that will approach you readily, ears up, and sniff at your outstretched hands. A horse that will drop its neck while you're next to it is almost always submissive. Avoid standoffish horses, especially ones that lay their ears back or roll their eyes. These are the horses that are going to make you look like an ass, and usually fairly early in the day. So pick out a nice horse, and then take a few minutes letting it get accustomed to your smell and your actions.

You usually mount the horse from its left side. Slide your left foot into the stirrup, grab the pommel with both hands, and swing your right leg up and over the saddle. Don't hop to get to the stirrups; the stirrup length is easily adjusted by sliding the strap through the circle clasp. Hopping excites the horse and makes you look silly – not a good combination.

Horses respond to pressure, whether it's applied to their sides or head/neck area. You need to apply this pressure through your legs or through the reins, but many beginners apply too much force, resulting in what seems like unpredictable horse behaviour. In reality, you're the one who's being unruly. Most riding horses are trained to respond to fairly subtle pressures, and strong yanks and kicks just get them worked up. Apply pressure lightly, either with the reins or your legs. If the horse doesn't respond, let off and then add a little more pressure, but move up gradually. Remember, the horse weighs a thousand pounds more than you; you're asking it to move, not telling it.

Trotting, loping and galloping can be brutal on the inexperienced rider and his nether regions. Instead of bouncing up and down on the saddle (which also bothers the horse), stand up in the saddle, which takes the pressure off you and the horse. This will allow you to bounce in rhythm with the horse's gait. It might tire your legs, but it's easier on you both.

Pull back on the reins to get the horse to stop, making sure the muzzle goes down, but don't apply too much force. Forcing the horse's muzzle down too hard will sometimes result in bucking, or a sudden stop that will send you flying over the handlebars into a hedge or, even better, a steaming pile of horse muck.

MAN ABOUT THE HOUSE

Solder copper pipes

'Ten minutes,' I told my wife, heading down to the cellar with my plumbing toolbox. Our old water boiler had basically disintegrated, but I reckoned I could install the new one with a few simple twists of a wrench. Upon further inspection, I saw that the new water heater was taller than the old one; I was going to have to cut the pipes and re-solder the old fittings onto the cut pipes. Not a problem, I said to myself, breaking out the torch. A piece of cake.

Well, almost. Four hours later my cellar looked like a loading bay on the Nostromo. Little geysers of steam and water hissed out at unpredictable intervals, pools of cold, clear fluid dotted the floor, and hunched in the corner was a creature who bore more than a passing resemblance to a pissed-off alien. Yep, that was me.

Soldering copper pipes is actually very easy – if you do it in a dry system. The problem I faced when connecting my new water heater was simple: I was working in a closed plumbing system. Water pipes retain drops of water even after you shut off the main valve, and when you apply heat during soldering, that water turns into steam. Steam builds up pressure in the pipes, which then blows the solder back out of the seal, and you end up with water leaks. Little, tiny, infuriating leaks.

If you're working in a closed system – and you probably will be – first shut off the main water valve, then open up every tap in the house so the steam can dissipate. Some people even shove chunks of white bread inside the pipe before soldering wet lines; the bread soaks up the water, reducing steam (the bread dissolves once the water is turned back on).

This has a moderate success rate, since the bread is damp and still produces some steam. Better to just open up the taps and heat the pipe with a propane torch until the steam disappears. You'll need a pipe cutter, torch, solder, flux, and sandpaper to make a good soldered seal. All are available at DIY stores for minimal prices, with the torch costing £10–£20. The pipe cutter has to be sharp, since dull cutters often warp the pipe, which in turn forms an imperfect seal with the fitting. Torch gas can be either regular propane or MAPP gas, which is more expensive but burns hotter. If you're using old flux, make sure it isn't lead-based, since this can cause water contamination. All modern flux is lead-free.

Use a rotary pipe cutter to cut the pipe. You can also use a hacksaw, but the cut won't be as smooth. Once you've cut through the pipe, sand the end with sandpaper. This removes burrs and increases surface area, which helps the solder attach to the pipe and

cont.....

connection. Apply flux to the end of the pipe(s) using a small brush. Flux is an acidic paste that cleans and primes the copper prior to soldering, and it should not be applied with your finger. I once lost my brush while plumbing my house and used my finger instead; after a day or so my finger had swollen so much that it looked like one of those Gladiators-style foam hands so beloved of ITV-watchers.

Once the pipe is cut, sanded and fluxed, insert the fitting. You may have to use a slip coupling if you can't fit a new fitting into the rigid plumbing system (these look the same as normal coupling but don't have interior stops).

Unroll the flux, light your blowtorch, and heat up the fitting. The hottest part of the flame will be right at the end of the blue cone. Heat the middle of the fitting, not the actual seam. Done correctly, the solder will flow toward the hottest part and suck into the fitting. You can almost always tell if you've formed a watertight seal, since the solder will circle the pipe and virtually disappear once you touch it to the seam. If it doesn't, keep heating the fitting. You'll know you're hot enough when the solder is sucked right off the tip.

Test an electrical socket

Of all the major trades, I find electrical work to be the easiest, both physically and mentally. Yet many people shy away from electrical work, refusing to even pop open the breaker box when the lights go out. While accidents still occasionally happen, modern electrical systems aren't anything to be frightened of as long as you follow some simple safety rules. Just turn off the power, make the repair, and turn the power back on. If you ballsed it up, the breaker will pop, and then do it all over again.

I like to think of electricity as a river, with many dams, locks and mill channels along its course. The actual wire is the main channel, with the switches acting as locks and the outlets, or plug sockets, serving as channels where the energy is harnessed. If we can wreck this comparison a bit further, the breakers (or fuses, in older houses) are the dams that can cut off the flow.

First you need to locate your circuit breaker box. This is usually in your cellar, under the stairs or in the utility room, and almost always on an outside wall. Open up the outside cover to reveal rows of fuse breakers, which should be labelled on a room-by-room or appliance-by-appliance basis.

If you want to work on a faulty plug socket in the master bedroom, just shut off the appropriate breaker. Then go and check the lights and outlet socket to confirm that the power is off. Many houses will have separate breakers for the lights and sockets in one room.

If the breakers or fuses aren't labelled, plug a radio into the outlet you want to work on, pump up the volume, and flip the breakers until the house goes quiet. To be really safe, use a pencil-style electrical tester to check the outlet. These light up if there's any electrical current present.

Adjust sticky or crooked doors

Sticky, crooked or loose-fitting doors can be irritating, and in the case of exterior doors, that cold draft can add hundreds to your heating bill. To counter this, some people resort to extra layers of weather-stripping or even shave the protruding edge off the existing door. But unless your house is located on the edge of an old coal pit, your house probably hasn't shifted enough to make either approach necessary.

A few minor adjustments will usually sort things out. If the door is dragging on the ground, your hinges may simply be worn out. Lift up on the handle; if the door moves up more than half an inch, you've got worn-out hinges. Tap out the metal rods between the two sections of hinges, remove the door, and unscrew the old hinges. Bring them with you to the hardware shop, buy new ones, and reinstall.

If the door sticks on the side, you might need to shave a bit off the corners of the door frame. But before you do this, try an old but effective trick: make sure the hinge screws are tight, then simply wedge a magazine or cheque book in the jamming spot for a week or two. This is often an easy cure for those slightly wonky doors.

To fix big gaps or really jammy doors, you'll need to adjust the position of the door inside the slightly larger door frame. Use a flat bar and a piece of wood to remove the interior moulding around the perimeter of the door, carefully prying it off so you can reuse it. Once the moulding is removed you'll see wedges on each side of the door, typically three sets per side between the studs and door jamb. By adjusting the thickness of the wedges, you can move the door inside the rough opening, squaring it up for perfect fit. You may have to cut out the finishing nails that secure the doorjamb to the frame before you can adjust it.

Adjusting the door this way can be frustrating, but there's a simple trick for determining which shims to add or remove. Take a cardboard box and knock the ends out, then move the corners of the box as a model. This shows you how the door frame will move as you add or remove shims. Remember to remove shims as you add them on the other side, and vice versa. This can be a trial and error process.

Once the door is set properly, countersink a few finishing nails through the side of the doorjamb (on the non-door side of the doorstop). Then score any protruding shims with a utility knife and snap them off. Finally, set the moulding back in place and nail it. Sorted.

Sharpen a knife

A good, sharp knife is one of the most useful things you can carry in your pocket, but a dull knife is about as useless as tits on a bull. And, strange as it may sound, the most dangerous knives are also the ones with dull blades. That's because people tend to apply excessive force trying to cut through something with a dull blade, causing the knife to slip.

Most knives made in the past 20 years have stainless steel blades, which don't rust and are harder than regular steel. Unfortunately, they're also a bit harder to put an edge on. If you're working with stainless steel, plan on spending about twice as long sharpening as you would with conventional steel. On the plus side, stainless steel blades hold their edge longer than regular steel.

All knife blades are actually saws, with microscopic teeth. When these teeth become dull or bent, the knife will quickly lose its efficiency. The easiest way to keep an edge on a knife is by using a steel (a thin metal file with a wood or plastic handle). Press the blade against the steel just above the handle, at about a 20-degree angle, then pull the knife up and out while maintaining constant pressure. Repeat a few times, then move on to the other side. This will quickly straighten and sharpen the teeth on the blade edge. If you're butchering or whittling, a few strokes on the steel every 15 to 20 minutes will keep your knife sharp throughout the process. The steel straightens those microscopic teeth, narrowing down the cutting edge to a fine, perfectly aligned row.

After a while, however, the microscopic teeth wear down and disappear. When this happens, you need to use a whetstone to regrind the edge of the blade and create more cutting teeth. Most whetstones will have different grit sizes on both flat edges and one edge. Wet the stone (mineral oil is fine, but so is plain old spit) and slide the blade over the stone in a circular motion, starting with the coarsest side and moving to the finer-grained side. Wet the stone frequently; a dry stone is basically useless, because the steel dust plugs the sandpaper-like qualities of the stone.

Check the knife's sharpness by pressing the edge lightly against the back of your thumbnail at about a 45 degree angle. If it slides off, the blade is still dull. If it bites into the nail, it's sharp enough to work with. If you can shave hair off the back of your hand you've achieved an extremely fine razor edge, which is nice for a little while, but it will quickly wear down into a regular old sharp blade. Use the whetstone once or twice a year, saving the steel for daily or weekly sharpening depending on how often the knife is used.

Change and sharpen lawnmower blades

The day I bought my first sit-on lawnmower was a very proud day. It was big and shiny and had a beer holder built right into the dashboard, one of the major selling points. Of course, I simply couldn't wait to try it. My wife and I had recently had some building done out the back of our house, and had excavated lots of earth into the bargain, so our lawn resembled a minefield, but I didn't let that deter me. I reckoned I could weave in and out of the patches of grass, no sweat.

I think I made it about 15 feet before I heard a tremendous crash and a massive stone shot out through – not under but through – the mower blades. I shut the mower off, and with the expression of a bloke about to look at some X-rays he really doesn't want to see, peered underneath the deck.

You know, sometimes the new doesn't wear off something. No, sometimes the new just falls off it. Well, I'm hardly alone. I'd wager at least half of all riding and push mowers have nicked, dull or damaged blades. Badly damaged blades can cause the shaft to warp, which can actually ruin your mower's engine. Dull blades, while they won't damage the mower, tend to crush instead of cut, damaging the grass and resulting in an unhealthy lawn and a lot of wasted effort.

Unless the blade is badly damaged, you can usually remove it and sharpen the blade yourself. A flat file or grinding wheel both work, but I've found a power sander puts an excellent edge on heavy blades with a minimum of effort (it also works great for sharpening axes and hatchets, not to make myself sound like some oddball out of *Saw*).

Simply tip push mowers up to get at the blades with the air filter up to prevent oil from draining into the cylinder. While it's possible to work on a riding mower by simply raising the deck, you may want to jack it up and block it, or drive the front end up on some car ramps.

The blades are held in place by a nut on the bottom of the shaft, but you can't simply loosen it up, as the blade will rotate with the nut. While you can sometimes slip another wrench onto the shaft above the blade, it's easier to wedge a bit of off-cut plank or board under the deck, then turn the nut until the mower blade bites into the wood. If you have tandem blades, mark the bottom of each blade so you put them back in the right way. If you're buying new blades, bring the old ones to the supplier to ensure you get a matching set.

Drill convincingly

There are two keys to successful drilling: use quality bits, and operate at the right speed. This is especially important with hard materials, such as steel or concrete. A quality drill bit set will not only make drilling much easier, but it will also last a lot longer than economy-type bits. I've had cheap bits literally disintegrate when they touched metal – they weren't worth the plastic case they came in.

Given the right bit and drill speed, it's easy to punch holes through just about any material with a minimum of effort. Wood is the most common material for the average handyman, and it's also one of the easiest to work with. Wood bits, or paddle bits, have a flared end with a sharp point, with the size of the bit stamped right into the metal. On each side of the point is a blade that is designed to cut through wood.

You can always tell how sharp your paddle bit is by the size of the shavings; big shavings mean a sharp bit, while a bit that produces dust is boring, rather than cutting, through the wood. If you're working on material where appearance is important, make sure you drill from the finished side in. Wood bits often create an outward explosion of splinters and chips when they exit the board.

For holes larger than an inch in diameter, use a hole saw. These bits, which are cylinders with saw teeth on the bottom, screw directly into your drill and have a drill bit located in the middle. Use the slots on the side to pry the material out of the interior once you've finally drilled through the board.

Drilling through steel is slightly trickier. Again, quality bits are extremely important; the best of them have diamond tips and are made out of hardened steel. The most common mistake when working with steel is drilling too fast. Cut at the lowest speed setting, working up only slowly, adding a couple of drops of honing or cutting oil to reduce heat.

You can always tell if you're cutting at the right speed by watching the steel waste coming off the bit. A sharp bit, operated at the right speed, will curl steel off the bit in long, winding strings. When drilling stainless or tempered steel, both of which are harder than conventional steel, you'll need to drill pilot holes first, then work up to the final size bit.

Drilling through concrete requires a special masonry bit. These bits have a thick, short, triangular blade at the end of the bit, and are best used with drills that have a hammer function. These types of drills work like a sort of jackhammer, crushing the cement instead of cutting through it. A masonry bit used in conjunction with a hammer drill can quickly cut holes in cement, brick, or stone.

Operate a circular saw

When working with circular saws, it's essential to have a sharp blade. Dull blades create bad cuts and are dangerous to boot, since they can produce kickbacks (if you haven't experienced this, imagine the saw reversing direction in a split second). If your saw smokes or hesitates when cutting through a board, it's time to replace the blades. They're safer, and you'll get a better cut, too.

While circular saws are designed to make long, straight cuts, attempting even a subtle shift in direction can cause the saw to bind. The easiest way to get around this is to cut faster. Like a bloke who runs across a tightrope, it's a lot easier to stay on course the faster you go. Setting your blade depth just deep enough to make the cut will also help prevent binding. There's a setting on the side of the saw that adjusts the fence depth, which in turn regulates blade depth.

Another common problem occurs when making long cuts on a sheet of plywood or chipboard. As you cut, the hanging portion of the sheet will sag, causing the saw to bind. While you can sometimes hold the sagging section up with your free hand or a work bench, it's usually easier to just set the sheets on runners, with each side of the cut balanced and supported. Set the blade just deep enough to cut through the board, and if necessary run it right over the runners.

Another trivial but irritating problem occurs when the saw becomes unplugged halfway through your cut. Many times simple tension makes them come unplugged, other times the plug end gets caught on the bench or the far end of the cut in the board. To keep the saw running, tie the extension cord and the saw cord together using a normal overhand knot, and then plug them together. It's almost impossible to pull the cords apart when they're tied like this, and I rarely plug in any power tool, saw or otherwise, without taking a few seconds to ensure continuous power.

Split-free screwing

No, I'm not about to give you advice on your sex life. We're talking using screws properly without creating unsightly splintering. Screws work well to bind two materials together, and they have the added bonus of being a lot easier to remove than nails if you make a mistake. The downside is they're much slower to install than nails, and they have a tendency to split wood, causing unseemly cracks. Those cracks also lessen holding power.

All you have to do to avoid splits is drill a pilot hole first, which is simply a hole slightly smaller than the diameter of the screw. Clamp the pieces together first, drill your pilot holes, and sink the screws in. You might want to put a couple of screws in right away to increase holding power while you drill the remainder of the pilot holes. This is the old tried-and-true method, and it works just about every time. But it's slow, especially when you have to keep changing bits between the pilot and driver bits.

Another, faster technique is to clamp the edges of the wood before screwing. This method reduces the outward pressure on the wood grain, and since wood will always split along the grain, you get a quick, neat solution to the cracking problem.

FUN & GAMES

Tap a barrel

It seems like nearly every big summer social event with friends and family involves a keg or two of beer. Handled, tapped and set properly, keg beer supplies a steady stream of cold brew that bites into the back of your throat just like canned or bottled beer. Too many times, though, barrels produce piles of foam on top of tiny amounts of liquid. Or, when a carbon dioxide (CO_2) system is used, the beer comes out supersaturated with carbon dioxide. I still remember the absolutely excruciating headache that sidelined a couple of my best friends and me the afternoon of someone's stag do, all because the gas setting on the barrel CO_2 regulator was too high. At the end of the night we had so much carbon dioxide in our system that plants would burst into full bloom when we staggered past, breathing heavily.

A metal barrel of beer is basically just an overgrown fizzy drink can. Shake it, and it's going to foam and spray. It stands to reason, then, that the single most important thing in producing quality tap beer is to keep it as cold and motionless as possible. This means the barrel should be picked up and iced at least 24 hours before the big party. It takes a long time for the contents to settle down once they get shaken up, and foamy or flat beer has tainted many a back garden event.

You can never have too much ice on a barrel of beer. Just set the barrel in a container with a slightly wider diameter, and line the bottom with ice. Pack the sides and top with more ice, then cover with an old blanket. Drill a small hole in the bottom of the container to let the melt-water out; this prolongs the life of the ice that's not yet melted. It's literally impossible to get a barrel of beer to freeze by adding ice, but easy to underestimate how much ice it takes to keep a big jug of lager cold on a hot summer day.

Once everything is iced and settled down, it's time to tap the barrel. If you're using a ball tapper, simply line up the slots, push it down, and twist it. You might get a little spray on you, but that's okay – it drives the ladies crazy, apparently. You'll have to pump the barrel as the interior pressure diminishes, but try not to add too much pressure right away. No matter how careful you are, the first few glasses of beer are going to be a little foamy. Just pour the first stream of beer into a pitcher and let it settle.

Carbon dioxide barrel systems are the professional choice of pubs, bars and home brewers across the country. These systems have a refrigerator to keep everything cool, and a gas cylinder that injects CO_2 right into the barrel, eliminating the manual pumping required with a ball tapper.

cont.....

The problem most people run into when using this system is determining the right pressure on the regulator. The correct setting is 10–12 PSI for lower elevations, slightly less than that at higher elevations. Low pressure equals flat beer, while a high setting produces frothy beer – or, occasionally, normal-looking beer that produces one of those splitting headaches.

Since a barrel has internal pressure to begin with, set it about 3 PSI lower when you first tap it. Then adjust the pressure upward as the internal gases are depleted. If you have long supply lines running from the tapper to the barrel, add a little more pressure. For a foolproof method with clear lines, just start low and adjust the pressure upward slowly until the bubbles in the line disappear.

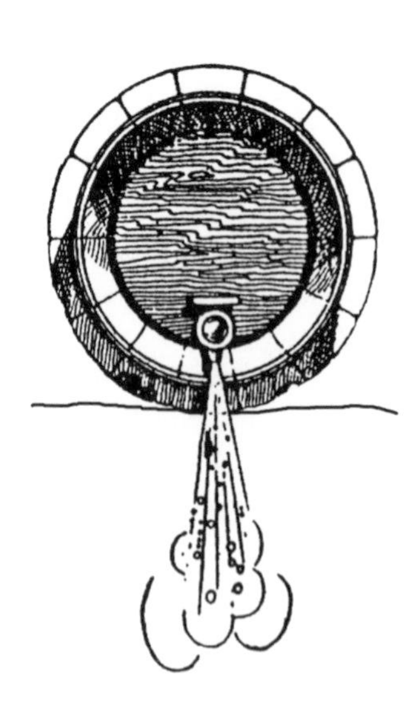

Shotgun a beer

Nothing says 'enjoy in moderation' like jamming a knife into the bottom of a beer can, popping the top, and pouring the entire contents down your throat in five seconds flat. But you've got to try 'shotgunning' a beer at least once, and it's better to do it without making a total prat of yourself

The problem most people run into when shotgunning a beer is trying to swallow it like they would a normal drink. This won't work; you'll just end up spitting the beer out and foaming at the mouth like a rabid dog. While conventional shotgunning wisdom dictates that you need to 'open up' your throat, this is a physical impossibility. Instead, you need to minimize the swallowing action.

You'll need a can of beer, unopened and at least cool, preferably not ice-cold but certainly not warm. Then, using a knife, ice pick, pen or other pointy object, punch a hole in the bottom of the can, and immediately cover it with your thumb. If you use a knife, give it a little twist to open up the hole. Then quickly pop the tab and tilt the can back as if taking a normal drink. With airflow unimpeded, the beer will flow straight out, without the typical gurgling, stop-and-go stream.

To minimize the swallowing action, press your tongue down and 'flex' the back of your throat. Done right, you'll immediately feel the throat area expand. It's close to a gagging action. Pour the beer back and relax your throat slightly; the beer should slide right down your gullet and straight to your stomach (and then, probably, to your overtaxed liver).

Sometimes you can't quite get it all down. If you're dealing with relatively inexperienced onlookers, crumpling the not-quite-empty can and throwing it to the ground victoriously will accomplish your goal (assuming looking, erm, 'cool' is the goal, not dehydration).

Down a shot without pulling a face

An unfortunate truth: almost any shot of cheap booze, poured straight off the shelf in a dirty bar, is going to cause your body to react in a 'get-it-out' manner. The particular reaction varies from person to person, from a mild pinching of the eyes and puckering to actual gagging and spit-ups. But unless it's a smooth drink and you're a few sheets to the wind, there's going to be an inherent reaction that can diminish your otherwise tough appearance.

Yet no matter how strong the shot it's usually not the taste that gets you. High-proof alcohol exists in both liquid and gaseous states, and the fumes caused by tossing a shot back often fill your mouth and nose with alcoholic gases. This is an unnatural and undesirable feeling; the common reaction is to shut your eyes and pinch your mouth, then breathe out from the back of your throat. This further volatizes the alcohol, which triggers the gag reflex and makes you look like a massive pansy.

Do not take a deep breath before downing a shot. Once the shot is downed a quick exhale will only give you a second shot of vapours. This after-effect is the real enemy when it comes to keeping a straight face and is exacerbated by lusty exhales and nose breathing. Avoid these, and you're halfway there. Exhale, then toss the drink back, getting it past your tongue as quickly as possible. Swallow immediately.

Now all you have to worry about is the fumes. Don't breathe in immediately, but simply open your mouth slightly. After a few seconds, breathe in shallowly through your mouth (not your nose!). This will keep volatization to a minimum.

The only real foolproof way to down a shot of whisky without flinching is to squirt some lemon juice into your mouth immediately before the shot. The resulting pucker closes everything off in your mouth, and the shot goes down as smooth as melted butter. Careful, though – what goes down also comes up, and the return trip isn't always so smooth.

Smoke a cigar

I remember well the anticipation before smoking my first proper cigar. It had been smuggled out of my dad's study drawer, and there were four or five of us waiting longingly to enjoy a fine smoking experience on a warm summer's evening. The general consensus? The £25 cigar tasted like total and complete shit.

The reasons for this are many, and none of them have to do with the initial quality of the cigar. Cigars are meant to be smoked within a few days of being removed from the humidor, and this one had been out a week or more, hidden in my bedroom. Additionally, we had smoked a strong cigar, which tasted bitter to our unconditioned palates. At that time I smoked half a pack of cigarettes a day, but even I couldn't stand the taste. Out of habit, I inhaled the cigar smoke – another big no-no.

If you want to enjoy a cigar, buy it right before you smoke it. This ensures the tobacco is moist and flavourful. Choose a mild cigar for the best taste; much like any connoisseur, you'll acquire stronger tastes only after you become used to the basic flavours. A good drink such as a scotch, brandy or a coffee liqueur helps to complement the flavour of the cigar.

Cut the cigar through the head [be ruthless, it won't hurt it] which is nearest to the label immediately before you smoke it. While you might see screen actors bite the end off a cigar, this usually rips the wrapping and causes the cigar to unravel. Use a sharp single- or double-blade guillotine cigar cutter to snip the head right before it reaches the thickest, main section.

Lacking a cigar cutter, use scissors or a sharp knife. Some people even use a pencil to enlarge the small hole in the end, but this method reduces smoke flow and might require a lot more suction than any bloke should really display in the company of other men. In fact, some people cut the cigar at a 45-degree angle to increase the amount of smoke. If you use a knife, cut completely around the cigar and then pull the end off. Dull blades and slow cuts compress the end of the cigar, resulting in reduced smoke flow. If your cutter is dull, just leave the cellophane wrapper on for a cleaner cut.

Light the cigar with a match or butane lighter, sucking from the cut end and rotating the cigar as you apply the flame. Repeat this rotation as you smoke. Since the cigar is tobacco from end to end, you can smoke it right down to the nub, but it often starts to taste ashy when you get down to the last couple of inches and things begin to get a bit beyond it. You never saw Hannibal or Arnie get that desperate while wasting some scuzballs or commies, did you?

Shuffle and deal cards like a pro

A sloppy deal during a game of cards is bound to piss some people off, whether it's a penny-ante game of poker or a £20-per-hand game of blackjack. Inadvertently flashing the bottom of the deck while dealing, spilling the cards all over the floor during the shuffle, or ignoring basic dealing etiquette isn't cool, and the people you're playing against aren't going to be very impressed. Done right, a thorough shuffle and level deal evens the playing field; done incorrectly and it's like the shop assistant scratching off your lottery ticket after you buy it.

The best way to evenly distribute the cards is to combine two or more techniques, usually a fine and a coarse shuffle. A coarse shuffle quickly separates groups of cards, while a fine shuffle separates individual cards. Most casinos have to shuffle at least seven times to ensure randomness, but that's a lot of shuffling for private poker parties. A couple of overhand shuffles followed by two or three riffle shuffles produces a good, fast mix. If you're playing with a new deck, feel free to spread the cards out across the table and mix them up before the actual shuffle.

The overhand shuffle is a perfect coarse shuffle. Use your right hand to pick up the deck lengthwise, with your thumb on one end of the deck and your middle and ring fingers on the other end. Hold your left hand underneath the deck, slightly cupped. Relax your fingertips enough to let a few cards slip through your grip and into your left hand, where they'll rest against your fingers. Then move the deck forward and let more cards fall in front of those cards, until the entire deck is in your left hand.

Repeat the whole process a couple more times, then move onto the fine shuffle. A riffle shuffle has two main things going for it: it effectively and quickly randomizes the cards, and it also looks like you know what you're doing. An inexperienced shuffler usually means an inexperienced card player, a cue that crafty card sharps quickly pick up on. A riffle shuffle is relatively easy to master, but you'll want to practise for a little while before the big poker night.

Pick up a deck and square it up by tapping it on the table. Turn the deck lengthwise, with your middle and ring fingers holding the sides. Bend your index finger so the last knuckle is pressed against the middle of the deck, forcing the middle of the deck to bulge outward. Relax the pressure on your thumb, which will let the cards snap onto the table. The sound should resemble muted machine gun fire.

Stop when half the cards have hit the table, then pick them up with your left hand. Tap the edges to even that half, then arrange the two sections so they're facing each other at a slight angle. Use the same technique you used to separate the deck to let the cards flow into each other. Once the cards are gone, you can simply push them together using your palms, or better yet, bend them up into an arch, with your thumbs forming an overhead bridge.

cont.....

Slide the cards together enough so about the top third are in contact with the other half, then push down on the base of the cards with your palm and in on the sides. This is where the practice comes in; experiment with hand and fingertip pressure until the cards bend into an arch, then slide back together.

Once you're done dealing, offer the person to your right (who passed you the deal) the option to cut by sliding the shuffled deck over to him. If he doesn't want to cut (many people don't, but it's nice to ask) he'll just tap the top of the deck. If he slides off a section of the deck and places it on the table, place the other half on top of this cut section and deal. Do not shuffle again after somebody has cut the deck. Et voila!

Throw a good poker night

The most important ingredient of a good poker game is having compatible players. It doesn't matter if your friends are serious card aficionados, or if their card-playing skills are based solely on years of playing snap with grandma – you can have a good time playing with either group. The key is to avoid mixing the two, especially if you have one very good player matched up with a bunch of amateurs, or a table of card sharps and some grunt with wads of cash and a full complement of tells. Hard feelings are bound to occur in either of these scenarios, and that's not what poker parties are about.

After you get the right bunch of blokes together, get rid of the cash. It's always easier to pay for something with a cheque or credit card instead of cash, and poker chips work in the same manner. Have everyone buy in for a set amount, then distribute chips. Substituting chips for cash means faster games, bigger pots and a more relaxed atmosphere. Even professional poker players on cable television would be hard-pressed to bluff effectively with £1 million in crisp notes sitting in front of them.

Once these two essential tasks are complete, all that remains are the creature comforts. Poker tables are nice but by no means essential; comfortable chairs are also a welcome bonus. Poker nights are often a great excuse to have a drink, a smoke and a swear, so for domesticated men the draughty old garage or cellar might be a better fit than the kitchen table. The key is to form a relaxed environment that is free of inhibitions, which translates into bigger bets and faster games (it's a

cont.....

lot more fun, too). Drinks work in the same capacity, of course, but also consider having a pot of coffee ready for the end of the night.

If playing more than one type of game, make sure everyone knows how to play them before you deal (the dealer will call the game, unless you're playing a winner-take-all game like Texas hold 'em). Often the dealer will be the only one to ante, with people having to call the ante to stay in the game. This is called a pot game. Otherwise, you can always play standard poker, with everyone putting in an ante. The advantage of a dealer-only ante, or a pot game, is that a string of bad cards won't totally clean you out. You only have to get in when you deal, or when you think you have a decent hand.

Play blackjack

It was a Friday night in Manchester, and seven of us wandered into a casino well-oiled and primed to donate cash. Within half an hour only a couple of us remained, the other blokes having either lost all their money or been thrown out by security guards after violating house rules. My remaining friend and I were doing better, but only because we were following the most basic of blackjack rules. Yep – we flirted with the overweight dealer, and she in turn waved the guards off when we broke card protocol.

Actually, we also obeyed the most commonsense rules in playing blackjack (or pontoon, as it's also known). We didn't hit when the dealer had anything between a six and two showing (unless we had a total of under eleven in our hand), we split aces and eights, and we didn't bend our cards up or touch our money once we pushed it in for a bet.

No matter how much fun you're having, you should never lose money fast at blackjack. Blackjack and craps are two games in which the house does not have a definitive edge, and you're much better off playing blackjack than plunking coins into a slot machine – provided you know what you're doing.

Many people like to try to pick a 'hot' table, which of course is basically nonsense. It's much better to find a table where you can position yourself immediately to the right of the dealer. This means you'll be the last player to get a card, so you'll see the most cards before you decide whether to twist. Once you're in position, cash in for some chips. Get a load of

cont.....

chips; dragging out your wallet every half an hour or so can have a very sobering effect. Push your bet into the designated circle, and then don't touch it until the dealer takes it or adds to it.

All you need to do to win is get a higher hand than the dealer without going over twenty-one. If you go over twenty-one, you lose automatically, even if the dealer goes over later. Face cards are worth ten, and the rest of the cards are worth their face value. The one exception is the ace, which can be either one or eleven. It's your choice, and the ace value is arbitrary, automatically shifting from one (aces low) to eleven (aces high) to give you the best hand as you twist to take additional cards, or hits.

Both of your cards go face down. The dealer's cards will be split; one down, one showing. Do not bend your cards to look at them; pick them up and then set them back down. In nearly every casino, it's assumed that a bloke who bends his cards is trying to mark them, and they'll give you the boot on general principles. If you're lucky, you'll end up with an embarrassing warning first. Not so cool now, eh?

The dealer's face-up card dictates how you'll play each game. Face cards, which are worth ten points, make up the greatest collective portion of any deck (tens are worth ten points, too). The suit doesn't matter. To play blackjack effectively, you have to assume the dealer's facedown card is worth ten points. If the dealer is showing a two, three, four, five or six ('bust cards'), assume he has a twelve- through to a sixteen hand. The dealer must twist on anything totalling sixteen or less, and must stay on seventeen. Never take a card when the dealer is showing a bust card, unless you have cards totalling eleven or less and can't possibly go over. Following that simple rule will make you welcome at any blackjack table, and will also increase your winnings.

If the dealer is showing an ace, he'll offer insurance, and you can bet half your original bet. If the dealer's down card then turns out to be a face card, you win two to one. Any card other than a face card and you lose it all. Avoid insurance – it's a sucker bet.

To indicate you want a hit, tap the table with a finger or your cards, or say 'Hit me'. When you want to stick, turn your cards horizontally. The dealer may still ask you if you want another hit; just shake your head or say no.

Splitting cards is a good idea on a pair of eights or aces; neither pair makes a great hand in itself, but is worth eighteen or twenty-one, respectively, when split and paired with a face card. You only get one hit per card when you split. Just spread the cards apart and put your original bet under one card, and the same amount under the other card. A total of twenty-one on a split does not pay out three to two, like a regular blackjack does. Splitting makes the most sense when the dealer has a bust card.

Build a spud gun

These things are wicked, and aiming one at a person is not very different to pointing a real gun at somebody. I remember vividly when a friend smashed a dent in someone's car panel with a well-placed tater. Spud guns are great, if slightly juvenile, fun, but they move fast and they hit hard. Be careful, and never point it at a person, animal or anything expensive and not yours.

For a few quid you can purchase all the materials and a sack of spuds, and in return you get a weapon that can launch Sir Walter Raleigh's finest at over 200 feet per second. This is noble, not to mention cheap, entertainment.

There are three basic parts to any functional spud gun: the barrel, the combustion chamber, and the igniter. These can be modified slightly, so feel free to experiment. Once you have everything, simply glue them together with PVC cement.

SPUD GUN PARTS LIST

1. A 24-inch length of 1½ inch or 2 inch PVC pipe (barrel)
2. A 12-inch length of 3 inch or 4 inch PVC (combustion chamber)
3. A reducer coupling to connect the barrel and combustion chamber
4. A threaded end cap and female bushing for the end of the combustion chamber
5. A couple of screws (optional) and a BBQ lighter
6. Spuds
7. Aerosol hairspray or a propane torch

Use primer and PVC glue to connect all the fittings, and make sure you do a good job, since leaks will lessen the power of launch, and can cause flames to spurt out the side of the combustion chamber. File down the muzzle so it's sharp, which will help cut the spud down to a perfect size when you load it up. Attach the igniter wire on the BBQ lighter to the screws so that a spark crosses when you pull the trigger. If there isn't a spark, move the screws closer together.

Just like an old Napoleonic cannon, load the spud from the muzzle, forcing it down the barrel to a point just above the combustion chamber. Use a stick or pipe to push it down to the base of the barrel. It should be a tight fit, since loose spuds don't go very far. This is where the filed edges of the barrel can be used to cut bigger potatoes down to the perfect size.

Once the spud is loaded, unscrew the end cap and give the combustion chamber a shot of propane or aerosol hairspray. You'll need to experiment a bit to get the right air/gas mixture; start out on the low side and work your way up. Quickly screw the end cap back on to seal the gases, aim the gun somewhere safe, and hit the igniter. Boom! Not exactly opera-night entertainment, but cracking fun nonetheless. Just be careful with it!

Open a bottle without an opener

Desperate for a swig but got no bottle opener handy? Usually all you need to open a beer bottle is to rest the edge of the cap against a hard surface and hit it sharply with the heel of your hand. A roadside kerb does the job nicely. Your wife's new solid-oak worktops are probably not such a good solution.

Wine bottles are a slightly more difficult proposition. If you don't have a cork puller, you can twist a screw into the cork (the wider the thread the better) and use pliers to pull on the screw and remove the cork. This takes a bit of muscle – traditional wine openers don't operate on a fulcrum system for nothing. If you don't have pliers or a screwdriver handy, a 'coat hanger' screw (usually brass, threaded on one end and curved on the other; often they're also used to hang plants from ceilings) can be twisted in and pulled out by hand. Use a screwdriver and a countertop as an improvised fulcrum system. This system works with both traditional and plastic corks.

MEAT & FISH

Grill a steak

It's not easy to cock up a good steak on the grill. If you cook a decent-quality steak (sirloin, rump or rib-eye) anywhere from medium-rare up to medium-well, you need only a sprinkle of salt and pepper to enhance the natural flavour. The only real way to spoil a good steak is to overcook it, yet that happens a lot more than it should.

There are two theories on how to cook a steak on the grill: hot and fast or slow and steady. Hot and fast works great to seal in the juices while crisping the outside, resulting in a tender, juicy steak. This method involves slapping the steak down on the grill right above the flames, then cooking it for five to seven minutes on each side. The problem with direct grilling is that the heat on many grills is uneven, resulting in patches of steak being grilled to a crisp. It's also tough to get the inside cooked thoroughly, since the searing keeps the heat from penetrating to the middle of the steak.

Slow and steady cooking, or indirect grilling, will produce a more evenly cooked steak. Adherents of this method use an elevated rack, or just push the steaks to one side of the flames, and keep the lid closed to create an oven-like environment. The problem with indirect grilling is that the juices often run off the steak as it heats, and you lose the charring and retention of natural juices that make a good grilled steak so tasty.

The best way to get an evenly cooked steak with full flavour is to combine the two methods. Quickly sear the meat on each side for a minute or two to char the edges and seal in the juices. Then remove the steak from high heat with tongs – forks and skewers release juices when they puncture the meat – and allow it to finish cooking under indirect heat. Use a meat thermometer to make sure that each steak is cooked to the right temperature. Don't cut them open to check 'doneness' since you'll lose juices and flavour. For a medium steak, the internal temperature should be about 140–150°F.

Chefs routinely reserve the worst chunks of meat for those customers who order well-done steaks. The reason for this is simple – you can't taste flavour in a well-done steak like you can with a medium-rare steak. Drying out a perfectly good piece of meat on your grill, then slathering it with artificial juices like steak sauce or – God forbid – ketchup is a total waste of the poor cow that died for your heathen appetite. At least try your steak cooked medium. If you can't bring yourself to try some pink meat, just buy some tofu for your next BBQ. It's cheaper, and will taste about the same. You big nelly.

If you're working with tougher cuts, there are a few simple household marinades to loosen up even the stringiest piece of beef. Cola, red wine, lemon juice and vinegar can all be used to tenderize tough cuts. Just add equal amounts of water and allow the steak to marinate overnight. Italian dressing works wonders for naturally dry cuts, and is an excellent marinade for venison, which lacks the marbled fat of beef.

Smoke a fish

We're not talking some sort of experimental omega 3-based hallucinogenic technique here. Just good, tasty, honest cooking. There isn't a shop-bought mackerel in the world that can compare to hot, freshly smoked fish, and smoking is deceptively simple. You don't need a special smoker: a gas or charcoal grill works almost as well. It's a time-consuming practice, but also easy and strangely fulfilling.

Fatty fish work best for smoking. Trout, salmon, herring, cod and mackerel are often used. Whatever you use, catch or buy them fresh (within a couple of months at most), since fish that are frozen for long periods tend to suffer protein breakdown and take brine too easily, resulting in salty fish. You should leave the skin on, but if you have only skinless fillet you can just slip a piece of aluminium foil underneath the meat during the smoking process.

Brining is one of the essential parts of smoking. Many old-timers used to throw in liberal amounts of salt; the adage was to use enough salt to float an egg. Today, with modern refrigerators, that amount of preservative isn't necessary. I use about half a cup of pickling salt per gallon of water, along with some brown sugar, soy sauce and fruit juice, but all you really need is the salt. Steak the fish or fillet them, leaving the bones in and skin on. Then soak the fish in the brine for about 12 hours.

The fire used for smoking fish has to be, well, smoky. Start a good fire with dry wood, then let it burn down to the coals. Add green (freshly cut or soaked in water) wood on top of the coals, which will produce low heat and enough smoke to cause the neighbours to remove their delicates from the clothesline. If you're using a propane grill, use the lowest possible setting and just one burner, saving the coolest side for the fish.

Alder or fruit-tree (apple, plum, etc.) wood produces a mild, flavourful smoke. If you can get them, mesquite and hickory produce a sharper smoke. Soaking the wood chips before use helps produce more smoke, no matter what kind of wood chip you buy or gather. Sounds odd, but heat is your enemy here, at least to start with; high heat sears the outer edges of the fish and doesn't let the smoky flavour work into the flesh. Don't put the fish in the smoker until you've got the temperature down to about 140–160°F. Smoke the fish at this temperature for roughly six to eight hours, or until the meat has browned and is just beginning to flake. Then bring the temperature up to 180–200°F for an hour to kill any parasites. Heat can be controlled by standard methods, either by adjusting air intake or fuel load. Don't shut down the smoke outlet though; this causes the smoke to sour and produces a bitter flavour in the fish.

Smoked fish lasts a long time in the fridge. It's usually best to make it in large batches, considering the amount of time involved. It makes a good gift, too; wrap it in baking paper and newspaper and people will invariably ask where you bought that incredible smoked fish. One word of caution: if you're using your normal BBQ grill for smoking, the oils from the fish will probably accumulate on the bottom of the grill or smoker and cause whatever you cook next to taste fishy. To eliminate this, line the bottom of the grill with aluminium foil beforehand. When you've finished smoking fish, remove the foil and start a hot, clean (no smoking chips) fire. That should take care of all or most of the fishy smell.

Pickle a fish

Pickling fish is another old tradition that dates back to the pre-fridge or freezer age. While modern refrigeration makes pickling unnecessary for preservation purposes, pickled fish has a distinctive, pleasing flavour, and the acid in the pickling brine will dissolve bones, which means fine filleting of those bony fish isn't necessary.

In the refrigerator, soak one-inch cubes of skinned fish in a brine solution containing two cups of kosher salt per gallon of water overnight. Rinse the fish and add the chunks to a large pot of water containing about five cups of water and two quarts of distilled vinegar. Add onions, garlic, allspice, mustard seed, cloves, and pepper for flavour (add more spices as desired – it's tough to ruin pickled fish), then bring it all to a simmer for 15 minutes. Do not cold-pickle fish unless you want to risk having a tapeworm take up residence in your intestinal tract. While the tapeworm diet undoubtedly has the edge on Atkins, there's still that 20-foot tapeworm to battle once you reach your fighting weight.

Take the fish out of the pot and place on a baking sheet, and then put the chunks in the fridge to cool down. Strain the pot of boiling vinegar with a colander or cheesecloth, then discard the spices and set the liquid aside. Pack the fish cubes in clean, sterilized (boiled) glass jars, adding more onions, garlic, and maybe a bay leaf or a wedge of lemon.

Bring the strained stock back up to a boil, and then pour it over the fish cubes. Seal the jars, then refrigerate for a few weeks. Serve with rye bread or crackers, lots of cold lager and a fishing yarn or two. Unbeatable.

Season and clean a cast-iron skillet

Over the years I've eaten many memorable outdoor lunches, little impromptu meals cooked over an open fire near water. Invariably these meals include freshly caught fish, good company and a battered old cast-iron skillet. The food that comes out of these skillets rarely disappoints, and the skillets themselves are pretty much indestructible.

Sadly, these old-style pans have given way to stainless steel and Teflon-coated cookware, despite the fact that cast-iron skillets hold a steadier heat and are even easier to clean than modern non-stick pans.

The key to using a new cast-iron pan is the seasoning process. Simply coat the inside of the pan with an animal-based fat, such as lard or bacon grease, and bake in the oven (or over a campfire) for about half an hour at 350°F. Remove the pan, scrape out the grease and bake it for a further two hours. Allow it to cool, then wipe dry with a rag or paper towel. Do not clean the pan with detergents or abrasive pads, which will ruin the coating you just applied and totally defeats the object. Also avoid cooking acidic foods such as tomatoes or citrus fruits, which can cause the skillet to rust. Stick with high-fat, greasier foods for the first few uses. Let's be honest – this usually isn't a problem on most camping trips.

Cleaning a cast-iron skillet is so simple it seems wrong, or at least unhygienic. But all you need to do is fill it with hot water after you're done cooking, let it heat up a bit, then wipe it clean. Again, don't use detergents or abrasive pads, both of which will strip away that unique coating.

Hang the pan or store it upside-down to prevent rust. If you do see rust pockets, just warm up the pan and scour it clean (okay, okay – now you can use an abrasive pad), then re-season it.

Cook a drunken chicken

Not only does this sound cool, but it's also the best way to cook a whole bird on the grill. Plus, you have to open a beer to cook drunken chicken, and beers are a bit like tortilla chips; you can't stop at just one. You have to sip a cold brew or two while the bird cooks (it's an unwritten law). Another great thing about drunken chicken is that you don't have to constantly tend it. The beer does the cooking for you. Whoever thought this up is my hero.

For the best flavour, season the chicken well both inside and out. Putting the chicken in a large bag with spices and shaking it works great, but you'll want to do it outside. Women tend to get a little fed up with paprika-laced chicken juice flying around the kitchen. Now stuff a small potato or onion in the neck hole of the chicken, and pull the skin flap over it. Sounds rank but this will help keep the steam inside the bird. Finally, open a beer and drink about one-third to half of it – never use a full beer when cooking drunken chicken. A full beer will boil over, dousing the charcoal and – even worse – ruining precious and perfectly drinkable beer. Set the beer in a commercially available 'drunken chicken' can holder – about £2 from all good BBQ outlets – then set the chicken down on top of the beer, arse first. The beer steam will slowly work into the chicken.

You'll want to be able to close the grill lid, so buy a small enough chicken. A charcoal grill gives a superior taste compared to a propane-fired one, but make sure you position the coals around the outside of the bird. It takes about an hour or two to cook a bird this way, but don't worry about being bored.

You've got the rest of that twelve-pack to keep you company.

Food for thought

Well, that's it. No theories for nuclear fission or world peace, but some fun and maybe even some new things to try.

If something does work out for you, pass it along. Nearly everything in this book I've learned from other people. Some of the lessons weren't much fun, while others went down so well I wasn't even aware I was being taught. Those are the ones I remember fondly.

It's not a contest, with the bloke who knows the most being the biggest man. If you can slip somebody a tip or two when he's in a jam, and do it in a gracious manner, then you're going to have that person's quiet but deep respect, and probably for a long, long time. I know I reserve a special part in my heart for the good people who've brought me through some thick tangles with a smile and a nod, and I try to emulate that whenever I can.

It's not always easy, but it feels right when you do it. More than right; it feels like the sort of thing any decent bloke would do. But then you probably knew that already...

INDEX

i

j

k

l

m

n

o

p

Loved this book?

Tell us what you think and you could win another fantastic book from David & Charles in our monthly prize draw.

www.lovethisbook.co.uk

Pub Science To Impress Your Mates

Bobby Mercer

978-1-4463-0044-2

This is the ultimate science textbook that will answer all your craziest science questions they didn't teach you in school. From crushing beer cans on your forehead to cockroaches surviving a nuclear blast, this book has it all.

Bollocks! Why Didn't I Think of That?

Anthony Rubino Jr

978-1-4463-0043-5

This must-have guide will allow you to impress your mates with your newfound, fascinating knowledge of the clever inventions we could no longer imagine life without – from toilet paper to the Theory of Evolution.

Facts That Will Scare The Sh!t Out of You

Cary McNeal

978-1-4463-0041-1

Disturbing phenomena are everywhere we turn and this book is jam-packed with facts that will horrify you, yet entertain and educate at the same time. Features everything from the ugly truth about food and drink, to the human body exposed.